OPERATION PHAROS

First edition, published in 2001 by

WOODFIELD PUBLISHING
Woodfield House, Babsham Lane, Bognor Regis
West Sussex PO21 5EL, England.

ISBN 1-873203-65-9

Operation PHAROS

and the story of the
Cocos (Keeling) Islands

KEN ROSAM

Woodfield *Publishing*
BOGNOR REGIS · WEST SUSSEX · ENGLAND

*The first Spitfire takes to the air from the newly-built
steel runway on the Cocos Islands, 1945.*

*This book tells the remarkable story of the Cocos/
Keeling Islands in the Indian Ocean from the time
of their discovery in 1609 until they became fully
integrated with Australia in 1984. But it is mainly
written to record the achievements of a few
thousand men of the British Armed Forces who, in
great secrecy, constructed and operated a Royal Air
Force bomber base and Air Staging Post during the
latter months of World War II under the code name
of 'Operation Pharos', thus becoming the most
advanced of all the Allied air bases in the South
East Asia theatre of operations. Also given is the
history of the 11 RAF Squadrons involved.*

A Cocos Island evening, 1945.

Contents

Liberators lined up on the airstrip, 1945.

Acknowledgements

Apart from my personal knowledge of 'Operation Pharos', I have used many sources for my research.

My first source, concerning Captain Keeling, who discovered the Cocos/Keeling Islands, was obtained from *Letters Archaeological & Historical Relating to the Isle of Wight* by the late Rev. Edward Boucher James MA, Fellow of Queens College & Vicar of Carisbrook I.O.W. (1858-1892), collected by his wife.

The early history of the Clunies Ross family and their possession of the Islands was compiled from the Clunies Ross family archives for inclusion in RAF DRO's, now at the Public Records Office.

For the general war situation in the Far East, I am indebted to AJP Taylor's *Illustrated History of the World Wars*.

Other sources are: *Mutiny in the British & Commonwealth Forces 1797 - 1956* by Lawrence James; the 'Emden' incident is well covered by R.K.Lockner's *The Last Gentleman of War* and Jim Fails gives good coverage of the 1953 England to New Zealand air race.

I am grateful to the very many men who wrote to me having been involved in the Cocos/Keeling Islands operations, among them, John Johnson, Peter Byrne, Les Parsons, Roland Hammersly, Eric Moore, Arthur Lappage, John Behague, Doug Hatcher, Neil MacClean, John Traynier, Joe Carberry, Michael Gardener, Ed Grinter, Harry Widdup and others no longer with us.

By far the greatest amount of information I have used is from the Public Records Office, Kew.

Lastly my grateful thanks to Wing Commander Derek Martin, OBE, FR. Met. S.ARAeS who was Chief of Staff to Air Commodore Hunt during 'Operation Pharos', for his encouragement from the very beginning of my researches.

Ken Rosam 2001

Aerial view of the Cocos Island airstrip, 1945.

· Comments ·

"Like an emerald necklace on a blue silk scarf."

So said the pilot of a Catalina flying boat on first sighting the Cocos/Keeling Islands shortly after dawn one morning in the early summer of 1942. He had just completed a long and tiring 14-hour flight over the wastes of the Indian Ocean from his base in Ceylon.

"Like coming home."

Was the comments of the bleary eyed, two-man crew of a photographic reconnaissance Mosquito on safely returning to their Cocos Islands base, after completing a 2,000-mile round flight to the southern coast of Malaya in the summer of 1945.

"Our haven at the end of the rainbow."

The sentiments expressed by the Captain and crew of a Dutch manned Liberator bomber on returning from a shipping strike off the coast of Java in July 1945.

Village on the Cocos Islands 1945.

Part One

1609 – 1941

HERE LIETH THE BODY OF THE RIGHT WORTHY
WILLIAM KEELING ESQVIRE GROOME OF THE CHAMBER TO
OVR SOVERAINE KINGE IAMES GENRALL FOR THE EAS
ST INDIE ADVENTVRORS WHETHER HE WAS THICE BY
THEM IMPLOYD AND DYINGE IN THIS ISLE AT THE AGE
OF 42 AN 1619 SEPT 19 HATH THIS REMEMBRANCE
HEER FIXED BY HIS LOVEING & SORROWFVLL
WIFE ANNE KEELING

Fortie and two yeares in this Vessell fraile
On the rough seas of life did Keling saile.
A Merchant Fortunate A Captaine bould,
A Courtier gratious, yet (Alas) not Old.
Such Wealth, experiene honour & high praise
Few Winne in Twice soe manie yeares or daies.
But what the World Admird, he deemd but drosse
For Christ, Without CHRIST all his gaines but losse.
For him, and his deare loue, With merrie Cheere
To the holy Land, his last course he did Steere.
Faith serud for Sailes, the Sacred Word for card
Hope was his Anchor, Glorie his Reward.
And thus With gales of grace, by happie venter,
Through straights of Death heauens harbor he did
ENTER

CHAPTER 1

In the Beginning...

THE COMMENTS of the man who is credited with the discovery of the Cocos-Keeling Islands in 1609, are not recorded. It is known that Captain William Keeling was a merchant, seaman and adventurer, who made three voyages to the East Indies to acquire goods for the London markets on behalf of the East India Company, a Company which had only been granted its Charter a few years earlier in 1600 by Queen Elizabeth I.

On 12th March 1606 he set sail from England as the General in Charge of some 310 men. His small flotilla comprised: *Dragon*, a ship of some 700 tons; *Hector*, 500 tons; and *Concert* of only 115 tons. His Captains were William Hawkins and David Middleton.

The small flotilla made the long voyage down the west coast of Africa and around the Cape of Good Hope then northwards towards India. At Socotra Island near the Gulf of Aden, the ships parted company and Captain Keeling turned eastwards to call at Bantem on Java where quantities of pepper and spices were acquired.

The sailors of those far off days were brave and adventurous men who sailed their cockleshell boats into unknown seas at a time when much of the modern World remained undiscovered by Westerners. Using primitive methods of navigation, their charts often showed many blank spaces marked with the ominous words, 'Beyond this place be Dragons'.

Opposite page: Plaque to the memory of Capt William Keeling in the Church of St Mary, Carisbrook, Isle of Wight.

Returning through the chain of islands of the East Indies, they commenced the long haul across the wastes of the Indian Ocean towards the coast of Africa. Although there is no written record, one can assume that at some stage a lookout's familiar cry was heard reporting the sighting of a small island low on the horizon. As they slowly circumnavigated the island, a further call from the lookout's lofty position high up the mast, led to the discovery of a further group of small islands some 15 miles to the south.

There is no record that a landing was made on any of these islands, probably due to the heavy surf pounding on the outer reef and the vulnerability of their small craft to damage in those seas, so far from any other land. The islands were given the name of Keeling Islands and the first to be discovered still bears the name of North Keeling. Their position was 12°12° South by 96°54°East.

This archipelago of coral islands was later said to be the best example of a coral atoll the characteristics of which are: an island or islands within an outer reef in the form of a circle.

The discovery of these remote islands was made during the reign of James I of England (James VI of Scotland). It was only 30 years after Drake sailed round the world in his ship *Pelican*, later to be re-named *Golden Hind* by Queen Elizabeth I.

The Islands were later shown to be 1,758 miles to the south of Ceylon and 1,329 miles to the north of the Australian Continent. Captain Keeling returned to England in May 1610, having spent 3 years, one month and nine days on the voyage. He later returned to India to take up an appointment as head of the Army but, when his application to return to England to collect his wife was refused, he resigned and on his return to England was appointed Captain of Cowes Castle on the Isle of Wight, where he died on 19th September 1619. He was buried inside the Church of St Mary's in the Parish of Carisbrook on the island and his last resting place is marked by a stone slab bearing the Keeling coat of arms in brass.

His wife, Anne, caused a painted wooden plaque to be erected on one of 13th Century transition Norman pillars within the Church as a lasting tribute to his memory. The plaque may still be seen today and shows a representation of a single-mast wooden sailing ship with the sails furled and pennants flying. Three figures are shown on her deck and various Latin words are painted on the sails, pennants and hull. On the deck is an open Bible inscribed *Verbum Dei* – the Word of God.

Beneath the painting is inscribed:

"Heere lieth the body of the right Worthy William Keeling Esquire, Groom of the Chamber of our sovereign King James, General for the Hon.East India Adventurers, whether he was thrice by them employed and dying in this ILE deed at age of 42.AN 1619, September 12th hath this Rememberance heir been fixed by his loving and sorrowful wife Anne Keeling.

Fortie and two years in this Veffell fraile
On the rough seas of life did Keeling fail
A Merchant fortunate. A Captain Bould
A Courtier gracious, yet (Alas) not Old
Such Wealth, experience honour & high praise
Few winne in twice soe manie years or daes
But whaf the World Admird he deemd but drosse
For Christ. Without Christ all his gaines but losse
For him and his dear loue. With Merrie Cheere,
To the holy Land his last course he did steere
Faith ferud for Sailes, the Sacred Word for card
Hope was his Anchor, Glorie his Reward
And thus with Gales of grace by happier venter
Through ftraights of Death heavens harbor he did enter."

The discovery of these remote islands, so far from the western centres of trade, created little, if any, interest. They did not appear on any maps prior to 1609 and it was not until 1622 that a map drawn by Hessel Gerritsz showed them as 'Cocos Eylanden' and Arcano del Mare shows the islands as having been discovered by the English. In 1659 French and Dutch charts also refer to the 'Cocos Islands' but it was not until 1753 that a Dutch manuscript gave a detailed description of the islands and included a map drawn by Jan de Marre.

Variously known by seamen as the 'Southern Islands', the 'Keeling Islands', the 'Triangular Islands' and the 'Borneo Islands', the islands were finally called the 'Cocos Islands' by the Dutch, a name which applies to many similar palm tree covered islands throughout the East. In later years they were visited by James Horsburgh, a Hydrographer of the East India Company who recorded the whole group as the 'Cocos-Keeling Islands'. One of the islands is still known as 'Horsburgh Island'.

The islands remained unoccupied for over 200 years following their discovery until, early in 1825, the French brigantine *Mauritius* hit the reef on Direction Island and capsized. Captain Le Cour and his crew struggled ashore and were rescued a few months later. Captain Driscoll of the British ship *Lonach* called at the islands on 24th November 1825 and reported the remains of the wreck. A mast, bowsprit and a wooden barrel were seen and a large rat population was also noted.

With a growing number of ships crossing the Indian Ocean, the Cocos Islands were somewhat of a problem to navigation. They were low down, rising to just a few feet above sea level and surrounded by strong currents and treacherous reefs. On 15th December 1826 the English brig, *Sir Francis Nicholas Burton* was wrecked on West Island and a number of lives were lost and in 1834 The brig *Earl of Liverpool* was wrecked on North Keeling Island and lost her cargo but her crew were saved.

So tiny and remote are they that, in 1827 a Dutch corvette, the *Anna Paulowna* was sent from Batavia to inspect the islands, but was unable to locate them.

In latter days, visitors to the islands have confused them with the Cocos Islands associated with Pirates and buried treasure. They have been most disappointed on being informed that those particular islands have been identified as being located many thousands of miles away off the coast of South America.

CHAPTER 2

Alexander Hare and John Clunies Ross

THE KNOWN HISTORY of the Cocos/Keeling Islands really began when Alexander Hare and John Clunies Ross made their first visits prior to returning and establishing a settlement.

Alexander Hare was a colourful character, the eldest of four sons of a London Clockmaker. In 1805 he was working in Portugal as a merchant's clerk but in 1807 he left this employment and in 1808 moved to Malacca on the Malayan Peninsular where he had secured a position with the East India Company.

While in Malaya, Hare made the acquaintance of Stamford Raffles, who, in 1819, was largely responsible for the founding of Singapore and in 1826 was instrumental in establishing the London Zoological Gardens.

At that time Raffles was Agent to the Governor General of the Malayan States and Hare apparently made a good impression on him.

The Napoleonic Wars were raging in Europe and Britain was assuming control over much of the Dutch East Indies in order to prevent them from being taken over by the French. For this purpose, Stamford Raffles obtained the permission of Lord Minto, the Governor General of India, to attempt the occupation of the Netherland East Indies.

Taking Hare with him, Raffles successfully accomplished his task. Among the possessions acquired was the Sultanate of Bandjarmasin on the Island of Borneo which had been abandoned by the Dutch. In 1811 Raffles became the Governor General of Java and in 1812 he appointed Hare as the British Resident in Bandjarmasin where he worked closely with the Sultan in reducing piracy and opening up the sea lanes to regular traders.

Alexander Hare negotiated a treaty between the Sultan and the British East India Company as well as feathering his own nest by acquiring from the Sultan the sovereign rights over 1,400 square miles of land. In 1815 Raffles promoted Hare to the position of Political Commissioner-General of Borneo. He set about creating profitable plantations of sugar, pepper and coffee for the Sultan, the East India Company and himself with the help of a number of staff supplied by Raffles and some 3,000 Javanese convict labourers. As a sovereign prince he struck his own coinage, had his own flag and became the first Englishman to be known as the 'White Rajah of Borneo'.

It was during this time that Hare met the young Scotsman, John Clunies Ross and gave him various employments including that of Bandjarmasin's Harbour Master.

The Borneo Estates were not a success, possibly because Hare began to spend considerable periods away from his plantations pursuing his own pleasures. During the next six years his empire began to crumble.

In 1813 Lord Moira was appointed as Governor of the Malayan States and the following year Britain and the Netherlands signed a treaty of friendship which gave back to the Dutch many of their former possessions in the East including Java and Borneo.

With the Dutch again in possession of Borneo, the Sultan of Bandjarmasin refused to honour his treaty with Hare and made a new one with the Dutch. The East India Company also abandoned him and Hare began petitioning the Dutch for compensation for the loss of his lands, but without success.

During his travels, Hare had acquired a harem of some 43 women and their 27 children together with 42 male slaves. It is believed that these had been given to him by a grateful Sultan for clearing out the nests of pirates around his coasts.

At that time the owning of slaves, particularly in the East, carried no stigma but in the West public opinion was turning. It was already illegal to own slaves in any of the British Dominions and, as Hare intended to go to South Africa, he sought out his friend, Stamford Raffles, and obtained from him papers of manumission in respect of his slaves. These would show that technically they were free people and would facilitate his entry into that Dominion.

When he had obtained the necessary papers he went to Java. He made such a nuisance of himself with his many complaints in respect of his pleas for compensation over his lost estates that in 1820 the authorities expelled him from that country.

With his brother John and a large retinue, Hare boarded the brigantine *Borneo*, which was captained by John Clunies Ross, and sailed to South Africa where he moved into a large farm near Capetown staying for several years.

The Clunies Ross family history shows that, following the ill fated rising of the Scots in 1715, Alexander Clunies Ross of the Clan Chattan in Sutherlandshire (who was to become the Great Great Grandfather of John Clunies Ross, the first 'King of the Cocos Islands'), was forced to flee from his estates and sailed from Montrose in 1716 with his wife and two sons, first to the Orkney Islands and then to Yell, one of the Shetland Islands.

The elder son, James, married a Norwegian girl, Catherine Plapen and they moved across to the main island of Zetland where their son John was born. John later married a distant cousin, Catherine Clunies and they also had a son whom they named John. In due course John married another member of the Clunies Ross family and in August 1786 they became the parents of John Clunies Ross, the first 'King of the Cocos Islands'.

The young John Clunies Ross was apprenticed to the Greenland Whale and Fisheries Company and later he transferred to the Company's South Seas Department. In 1813, while at the port of Coupang on the island of Timor, he was given command of the brig *Olivia* by the British Java Government and set sail for Batavia where he met Alexander Hare.

Hare asked Clunies Ross to superintend the construction of various projects that he was undertaking and it was while he was carrying out this work that he, with his brother Robert, constructed the 428 ton brigantine *Borneo*.

Alexander and John Hare and John and Robert Clunies Ross formed a business partnership to trade throughout the Far East, collecting coffee, peppers and spices for sale on the London markets. The partnership was not very successful but survived for a number of years. While Hare was temporarily settled in Capetown John Clunies Ross continued to ply between London and the Far East. Early in 1825, Clunies Ross called at Capetown where he met Hare who asked him to investigate Christmas Island as a possible site for a settlement.

John Clunies Ross collected a cargo of pepper and commenced the return journey through the Sunda Straits between Java and Sumatra ready for the long haul across the Indian Ocean towards the coast of Africa. On reaching Christmas Island he was unable to land because of the heavy surf and carried on to the Cocos Islands, which he had not previously visited.

Arriving off the islands on the 6th December 1825 he found a passage through the reef into the placid waters of the lagoon where he was able to anchor in safety. On going ashore he made a preliminary survey and found that the islands were uninhabited. They were densely covered in coconut palm trees and thick scrub. There was no fresh water but a few feet under the coral surface he found an abundance of drinkable water.

Clunies Ross thought that the islands appeared to be an ideal place for raising a family. With that in mind he dug some wells, planted a few seeds, some fruit trees and carved his initials on the trunks of some of the trees. He then resumed his journey to England, making plans to return with his family.

Meanwhile, life was becoming increasingly difficult for Alexander Hare in South Africa and he decided to take passage in the brigantine *Hippomenes*, which was commanded by Robert Clunies Ross, and return to the East to look for a suitable place where he could settle with his harem and slaves away from the prying eyes of a society with whom he was out of touch.

Sailing eastwards the, *Hippomenes* reached Christmas Island where, like Clunies Ross in the previous December, they were unable to land through the heavy surf. They put about and decided to try for a landing on the Cocos Islands where they arrived in May 1826 and found evidence of Clunies Ross's earlier visit. Hare decided that these isolated islands were an ideal place to settle. His retinue of slaves, together with large quantities of stores were ferried ashore and placed on the white coral beach of Home Island from where Hare watched as Robert Clunies Ross sailed off in the *Hippomenes*, leaving him to whatever the future held for him.

In London, John Clunies Ross decided to get government permission to make his occupancy of the islands secure and enlisted the help of Hare's brother John, a man of some influence, who agreed to take the matter to Mr Huskinson, the Colonial Secretary of the time.

During one of his visits to England, Clunies Ross had met and married a young woman by the name of Elizabeth Dymoke at Alverstoke. It is alleged that he met her when he was being chased by the 'Press Gang' and sought refuge in her father's house. He was becoming increasingly aware of his responsibilities as the father of five children and could see few prospects of securing sufficient means of independence in England. The House of Hare was suffering badly from a number of Alexander Hare's outstanding accounts with the East India Company and others. He decided to emigrate and try and persuade Hare to return to England and settle his affairs.

Having made the decision, he collected ten young Scotsmen of like mind and, with his family and mother-in-law, boarded the *Borneo* and set sail from the cold and damp of an English Autumn for the sun and warmth of a tropical island. They reached the Cocos Islands on 27th February 1827 and Clunies Ross was furious to find that Hare had established a settlement on Home Island and set up camps on most of the larger islands.

Clunies Ross set up his original camp on Pulu Gangsa (Goose Island), immediately to the north of Hare's main settlement but, as tension grew between the two men and their followers, he moved to South Island where he named his camp New Selma after a legendary ancient capital of the kingdom of Scotland.

The situation was not a very happy one as the two men were completely different in character. Hare wished to carry on acting as an island despot surrounded by his harem and slaves and Clunies Ross wished to use the islands as a trading post for the storage of spices, pepper, coffee etc.

The ten men that Clunies Ross brought to the islands were all tradesmen or apprentices, J. Munslaw was a boatman, George Brown a tailor and boatman, Thomas Deeley a carpenter, Joseph Bayley a carpenter, R.Steevens a blacksmith, J.Steevens an apprentice, C.Steevens an apprentice, Andrew Moody an apprentice, W.C.Leisky an apprentice, and J.B.Gray was an apprentice. In addition he brought Ivan Antonio, a Portuguese cook and two hired native servants. In December 1926 Henry Keld, a survivor from a ship wrecked on West Island, joined him. Alexander Hare had his slaves and in 1828 he was joined by two men from the *Hippomenes*, Norman Ogilvie, whom he employed as a supervisor, and Arthur Keating.

As time passed, Clunies Ross found that John Hare in London had been of no help to him. The islands were too small and remote from the seat of government for them to worry about. He persevered and eventually was able to present a petition directly to the King William IV, but even this failed. As a result of his persistence, a naval vessel, HMS Comet under the command of a Captain Sandiman was sent to the islands to try and settle the matter. Arriving off the islands on 18th February 1830 Captain Sandiman set up a Committee of Inquiry but no conclusive result was forthcoming and he sailed away leaving a frustrated Clunies Ross and a disgruntled Hare who had been trying unsuccessfully to negotiate with the Dutch.

It was hardly surprising that neither of the two men had been able to interest any of these governments in a group of islands so small and remote and with a population which had grown to only 20 white men and 150 natives. The natives had come from Java, Sumatra, Borneo, Bali, Celebes, Africa, India, New Guinea and China – an extraordinary mixture – which was accounted for because the crews of the two ships, *Borneo* and *Hippomenes* both contained a mixture of men from many races and the women of Hare's harem were recruited from various eastern nations.

In 1836 Clunies Ross went to the Island of Mauritius where he unsuccessfully tried to persuade the Governor to take over the Cocos Islands. During his absence Captain Robert Fitzroy, a Royal Naval Officer and Charles Darwin visited the Cocos Islands in HMS 'Beagle' during their epic voyage round the world.

During his visit, Captain Fitzroy carried out a detailed survey of the waters around the islands on behalf of the Board of Admiralty. Copies of his charts, with various amendments, were still in use up until the outbreak of World War II. He later became a Vice Admiral, the Member of Parliament for Durham and in 1843 the Governor of New Zealand.

Charles Darwin was making a study of the formation of coral reefs and it was largely on the observations that he made during his visit to the Cocos Islands that he based many of his theories. Darwin met Alexander Hare but was not impressed by him .In his diary he refers to him as being a worthless character.

John Clunies Ross built a small factory concentrating on the island's natural resources by collecting and processing the coconuts and calling his business an oil factory. The small factory and processing plant was worked mostly by the women of Hare's harem and the enterprise proved remarkably successful considering the differences between the two men. In 1829 the *Borneo* shipped several tons of oil to England.

It was over the question of slave labour and the treatment of the coloureds that Clunies Ross and Hare were often at loggerheads. Hare continued to treat his workforce as slaves whereas Clunies Ross treated his labourers as free men. As a consequence, many of Hare's slaves deserted to Clunies Ross, who was only too willing to receive them and increase his labour force. The majority of Hare's slaves were women while Clunies Ross's group comprised many lusty young men, deprived of the company of women. In the island's folk lore there are many stories of midnight swims between the islands separating the two parties, of hasty flights and even kidnapping, all of which aggravated the discord between the two men. Hare tried to persuade the young men to leave his women alone, even attempting to bribe them with gifts of meat and rum, but to no avail.

In this way Clunies Ross's small band of settlers increased while that of Hare's diminished and his influence decreased. The final disaster came to Hare in 1836 when one of his male slaves led a group in wholesale desertion to the Clunies Ross camp and the *Borneo* returned to the islands with more settlers.

This brought to an end Hare's attempt to realise his long cherished ambition to become the Monarch of an Eastern Paradise amidst the luxurious setting of a tropical island. He moved from island to island within the group with his retinue growing progressively smaller, until finally he settled on the small islet known as Prison Island.

Within a matter of months, Hare gave up in despair and left the islands for Batavia and then on to Singapore. Some reports say that he died 10 years after leaving the Cocos Islands, others that he died in Java in 1834. The latter date cannot be correct as Charles Darwin noted that the two met on the Cocos Islands in 1836.

So ends the saga of one very colourful character who was closely associated with the founding of the Cocos Islands community. The fact that throughout his life Alexander Hare did not always conform to the pattern of behaviour that others of a later age might expect, does not detract from his many achievements during a turbulent period of history.

Following the departure of Hare; John Clunies Ross moved his small group to Home Island, where he assumed control over the remainder of Hare's people. Many of his original Scots had left the islands but he had a number of Javanese seamen and with their help taught some of the islanders the craft of building sailing ships. The first was built on South Island and named *Harriet.*

Clunies Ross discontinued his plans to make the islands into a trading post and concentrated his resources on the growing and processing of coconuts in his small factory. Commencing with the export of whole coconuts to Mauritius and Singapore and coconut oil to Java, by the year 1837, ten years after he had first settled his family on the Cocos Islands, he had succeeded in recovering his original investment.

A group of Cocos Islanders, 1943.

CHAPTER THREE

John Clunies Ross 'King' of the Cocos Islands

WHEN ALEXANDER HARE left the islands, John Clunies Ross was then able to concentrate on developing the islands into what must surely have been one of the first workable socialist systems in the modern world - notwithstanding that he retained complete control and his word was law.

He enlisted the aid of his eldest son John George Clunies Ross and they developed a simple legal code, introduced a special Cocos Island money and produced a code of practice governing the living conditions of the work force. The fundamentals of the system were:

(a) Employment for all

(b) Free medical treatment

(c) Care for widows and the fatherless

(d) Optional retirement at 60 years of age on half pay

(e) A high standard of living

(f) A simple code of laws

The island kingdom comprised 27 coral islands and islets grouped in a semi circle around a shallow lagoon, the whole being surrounded by a reef beyond which was deep water. The largest, North Keeling Island, lay some 15 miles to the north of the main group.

All the islands were densely covered with coconut palms, a few iron wood trees and thick scrub. The only wildlife consisted of thousands of large but harmless land crabs, (which only inhabit the Cocos Islands and Christmas Island), numerous rats, centipedes, ants and locusts. The warm waters of the lagoon supported an abundance of fish and, although the islands were only 12° south of the Equator, the temperature was most pleasant, remaining fairly constant in the low eighties for the greater part of the year.

The were no Anopheles Mosquitoes, (later established as malaria carriers), unlike so many other parts of the Far East. The islands being so remote from the large communities of civilisation, the islanders remained relatively free from disease, although they were prone to the common cold and had little resistance to infection or disease brought in from outside the islands. It was for this reason that Clunies Ross made it mandatory that, should any islander wish to leave the islands, he or she could do so, but on no account would he permit them to return. This rule was strictly enforced.

There was little topsoil on any of the islands and when it was needed it was imported from Christmas Island. With no natural springs or rivers many wells were dug from which an adequate supply of drinkable water was obtained.

The surface of the ground on all the islands was uniformly level varying from three to ten feet above mean sea-level.

It was found that the South-East trade winds blew for some 300 days of the year and the rainfall was fairly light, usually in the form of showers lasting from two to twenty minutes, except when the edge of a cyclone passed nearby, when showers could last for several hours. The average rainfall was found to be 77 inches per year, the two seasons being October to March which was the driest and April until September, the wettest.

Although the Giant Manta Ray, Tiger Shark, Barracuda and Hammerhead Shark reigned in the deep waters beyond the barrier reef, within the shallow waters of the lagoon were smaller Basking Sharks, Coral Trout, Dog Tooth Tuna, Bone Fish, Spanish Mackerel, Trevally, Sail Fish and other species of tropical fish in abundance.

All the islands were given native names but the larger ones were usually known by their English names which evolved over the years to Home Island, South Island, West Island, Prison Island, Virgin Island, Rat Island, North Keeling and, later, Horsbugh and Direction Islands.

Clunies Ross was 41 years of age when he settled on the Cocos Islands in 1827 and was of a philosophical frame of mind with a firmly settled belief in Divine Justice. As the years passed he was able to develop his ideas and these were expanded by future generations of his family, turning the island enterprise into a very profitable business.

The women were largely employed as copra workers, either in the drying sheds or shelling the nuts. Some widows and older women were employed as midwives or on laundry work, but no woman was compelled to work unless she wished to do so, in which case work was found for her. At the age of 65 years any worker, male or female, could retire on half pay.

When the boys reached the age of 14 years they were taken into the workshops for two years and if they had the ability as craftsmen were retained there. A 9-hour working day was established, the hours being from 6 am to 8 am, 9 am to 12 noon and from 1 pm to 5 pm. Sunday was a free day. There was usually insufficient work for large numbers of technicians or skilled workers but numerous other types of work was found so as to maintain full employment, such as copra baggers, loaders, bush gangs, hygiene workers, cooks, road menders, house servants, store-keepers etc.

Among the skilled trades were masons, boat builders, blacksmiths, sail-makers, carpenters, and, in later years, electricians and engine mechanics All of these innovations were evolved over many years.

Clunies Ross introduced a monetary system into the islands, the Cocos Rupee. This was originally based on the Dutch Guilder in which all his trading transactions were carried out. The sterling value of the rupee was one shilling and eight-pence, (nine new pence).When Clunies Ross transferred his business to Singapore the rupee retained the same value. Initially the money was in the form of notes but between 1910 and 1913 coins made of ivorine were introduced. These were light and handy but could only be spent in the island's store. The reason for the introduction of this monetary system was to prevent the islanders purchasing drugs, firearms, ammunition, alcohol etc, from the crews of ships that visited the islands from time to time.

The islanders were encouraged to save and many did so, accumulating substantial amounts, which, in the event of their death were distributed among their surviving relatives. The Clunies Ross family did not encourage extravagance. Ordinary goods such as food or clothing could be brought in unlimited quantities but for goods such as jewellery an islander was only permitted to import such items once. Clunies Ross had seen the result of too much extravagance in other Malayan countries where many of the people were permanently in the hands of the money-lenders and shopkeepers as a result of incurring debts for jewellery, marriages and funeral expenses. On the Cocos Islands nobody was in debt.

Monetary rewards were not the only payment that the workers received. Each family was issued a free 150 lb. bag of flour every three months. There were also free issues of dhal, chillies, tamarind, pepper, turmeric, and coriander with additional issues of these ingredients on the occasion of a funeral. Rice, sugar, tea and coffee were sold at much below the cost price as were many other items.

It was because of the system introduced and practised by Clunies Ross and his descendants, that the inhabitants of the Cocos Islands were without doubt the best fed and healthiest community in the Far East.

To those who became acquainted with the living conditions of the Malayan and Indonesian people, this system had much to commend it. One reason was that it removed the incentive to economise on the buying of food, which leads to the deterioration of people's health.

The Clunies Ross administration strongly objected to the natives bartering or selling foodstuff as much of it had been supplied to them at far below the cost price. As it was, the supply of fruit, eggs, vegetables and fowls barely covered the islanders needs. One custom that made it difficult to keep poultry supplies at a reasonable level was the insistence of the natives on keeping one rooster to one hen, especially as many eggs were eaten by the numerous rats and land crabs which abounded throughout the islands.

Sunday was kept as a free day and most families went fishing, collecting firewood, coconut husks or coconuts for their own use. They were permitted to collect 120 coconuts per week from South Island and these were used to make coconut oil and soap for domestic use and for fire-lighting. They were also able to collect nuts from any of the trees on Home Island where the community resided and any fallen nuts which had commenced to sprout. The soft centre of these sprouting nuts was called 'tombong' and was an excellent food for babies and small children. Those who could not leave their home island on a Sunday were permitted to collect copra from the copra sheds.

On marriage the Clunies Ross family presented the couple with a house of a standard pattern and included items of heavy furniture. They were expected to keep the house in good order and repair but the replacing of structural timbers was done free by the estate who also paid for half the cost of building a boat, (Dukon), unless the maker built it himself, in which case he only had to pay for the materials. All such boats had to be used free of charge on the estate during working days, i.e. Monday to Friday.

Medical attention and medicines were supplied free and sick pay was given at the rate of half pay. In later years a Doctor from the Cable and Wireless Station on Direction Island visited Home Island twice weekly. Dental care depended on whether the Doctor was qualified to do such work, if not, there was usually an extremely competent native dispenser on the island who, although not qualified in any way, could expertly undertake extractions without the benefit of anaesthetic.

Venereal disease and malaria never existed among the islanders and the principal ailments, apart from dengue fever, were asthma and bronchitis. The skin diseases, which were always obvious in other parts of the Far East, were not found among the natives of the Cocos Islands.

Most of the Cocos Malays came from the Island of Java and were Moslems of the Shafii sect. In accordance with their custom, marriage was allowed on reaching the age of puberty, usually 13 or 14 years in the East. However, when Clunies Ross formulated his rules for the well being of his islanders, he put the age of marriage at 20 years for males and 18 years for females. Over the years this proved to be too exacting and was subsequently reduced to 18 years and 16 years respectively. As a result, both parties put in three or four years work before they married which could well account for the strong and healthy children found throughout the islands.

By overriding Moslem law, it would seem that Clunies Ross and his descendants conferred a great and lasting benefit on the natives of the Cocos Islands.

In later years the birth-rate steadily increased to 50 or 60 per annum and the children grew up in a healthy environment where there was no unemployment. They were guaranteed a full working life from the age of 13 or 14 years together with care for the rest of their lives. Widows and orphans were looked after so as not to be a burden on their remaining relatives.

This was the culmination of the aims of John Clunies Ross, which he laid down all those years ago and which generations of the Clunies Ross family maintained.

It was not always easy, either for the Clunies Ross family or the natives that they employed. As the size of the community increased the sale of copra alone could not sustain such a generous system of living and had to be supplemented from the Clunies Ross family's commercial interests from outside the islands.

John Clunies Ross died on Home Island in 1854 at the age of 68 years after an eventful reign of 27 years. He was buried beside his wife, Elizabeth, on the islands which had meant so much to him. His grave is marked by a slab of granite which had been brought from his native Scotland and suitably inscribed by island craftsmen. His achievements as a benefactor to a community for which he was responsible could not be surpassed.

One of the islands many legends says that when John Clunies Ross died, his Grandson, a boy of 12 years, was sent off in a boat to bring ashore the crew of the island's schooner to attend the funeral. On arriving at the schooner he found that the entire crew were waiting for him dressed in black and aware of the death of their Master, yet no one from the shore had visited the boat. They said that they knew of the death because when the Spirit departed from the body of their Master each of them had heard a loud rushing sound through. the air and had heard the wail of the passing spirit of their Chief.

John Clunies Ross was succeeded by his son John George Clunies Ross, who had been born in Stepney, a suburb of London, in 1823. He had been taken to the Cocos Islands when he was 4 years of age and had spent most of his adult life at sea. He had married a Malaysian woman of royal blood named Supia Dupong in 1841 and they had 9 children, 7 of whom were boys. The new 'King of the Cocos Islands' had been responsible, with his father, for devising a simple legal code for the settlement and later introducing the monetary system.

John Clunies Ross had been a prolific writer, as were many of his descendants, thus providing a source for latter day writers of the Cocos Islands history. In fact, when John Sidney Clunies Ross died in 1944, a mass of their writings and reports of the island's business going back to 1827 when the islands were first settled, were discovered in abundance, packed indiscriminately in drawers and boxes.

Early in 1945, when Lieutenant Colonel J. A. Harvey, M.A. became the Military Administrator of the islands, he was able to condense some of the accumulated files into a readable report which was published in the island's Royal Air Force Station's Routine Orders, thus giving the troops an insight to the history of the islands, which were to be their base while pursuing the war against Japan.

On 31st March 1857, three years after the death of John Clunies Ross, *HMS Juno* under the command of Captain Freemantle, RN dropped anchor in the lagoon. John George Clunies Ross was visiting Java at the time leaving his uncle, James Clunies Ross, in charge of the Estate. James was astonished when Captain Freemantle presented official papers showing that Britain was finally going to annexe the islands as part of the British Dominions and making John George Clunies Ross the 'Governor of the Settlement during His Majesty's Pleasure'. James Clunies Ross signed the papers on his nephew's behalf and *HMS Juno* remained for three months until Captain Freemantle met the man he had designated as 'Governor', which gave rise to a great deal of celebrating.

It was ironic that, after 31 years of unsuccessful petitioning, the Cocos-Keeling Islands were finally annexed by mistake. It was a further 30 years before the British Colonial Office admitted that Captain Freemantle had been sent to annexe the Cocos Islands in the Andaman Group in the Bay of Bengal, islands which had in fact already been annexed by Britain. But, due to a series of errors, Captain Freemantle arrived at the Cocos-Keeling Islands. The mistake having been made, the orders were never rescinded.

John George Clunies Ross was an able administrator having been involved in the running of the island settlement during the latter years of his father's life. He reigned for 18 years until his death in 1872 when his eldest son, also named George, succeeded him.

In 1876 the islands were placed under the administrative control of the Governor of Ceylon and ten years later, by an indenture dated the 7th July 1886, Queen Victoria granted the islands in perpetuity to George Clunies Ross and his descendants. At the same time the islands were made the responsibility of the Governor of the Straits Settlement for administrative purposes until, in 1903, they became part of that Colony.

By 1888 the native population had increased to 538 and the annual report of the visiting Straits Settlement officials showed that there had been no crimes committed during the previous seven years.

Early in 1892, a boat named the *Luigi Raffo* with an Italian crew was wrecked off the islands and the eighteen-man crew were rescued and taken ashore by the islanders. The Italians soon outstayed their welcome with their outrageous behaviour towards the island girls and on 29th February 1882, Clunies Ross put them aboard the island schooner, *The John George Clunies Ross*, with a crew of eight native-born islanders and a Norwegian. The boat was a good seaworthy craft with an experienced crew but it was never seen again. As the weeks went by and it did not return, it was assumed that the crew had been overpowered by the Italians who had then commandeered the boat and sailed it under a different name.

The islands were struck by cyclones four times during the last thirty years of 19th Century and again in 1902 and 1909, which laid waste many of the coconut palms on the plantations. These had to be re-planted in 1876 and again in 1909. As the coconut palm does not bear fruit for six years and becomes fully fruit bearing at ten years, these disasters were catastrophic to the island's economy and the establishment suffered huge financial losses.

When the cyclone of 1909 hit the islands on 27th November, it was accompanied by huge waves which flattened everything before them, causing the loss of some 800,000 trees and damaging or destroying 40% of the island's boats. One man was killed by a falling tree and another died of exposure.

The storm, and its aftermath, so damaged the health of George Clunies Ross, the third 'King of the Cocos Islands', that the following year he returned to England to recuperate. While in the United Kingdom he visited the Isle of Wight, where Captain William Keeling, who discovered the Cocos Islands, had originated and was buried.

While he was staying at Ventnor on the island, he became seriously ill and died on the 7th July 1910, leaving four sons and five daughters. He was buried in the Churchyard at Bonchurch where his body remained for 5 years. On the 8th February 1915 it was exhumed and placed on the schooner *Rainbow* which had been despatched from the Cocos Islands to collect the body for it to be re-interred in the family plot on the Cocos Islands.

On the death of his father, John Sydney Clunies Ross became the fourth 'King of the Cocos Islands' and adhered strictly to the policies which had been formulated and practiced by his predecessors over the years, proving to be a benevolent and fair leader of his people.

CHAPTER FOUR

The Sinking of the 'Emden' – 1914

DURING THE FIRST THREE YEARS of the twentieth century, a cable relay station was established on Direction Island. The cable ship *Anglia* was used to lay a cable from Rodriguez and Mauritius which connected with Africa and the *Magnus* carried the cable on to Batvia in Java. The *Scotia* took the cable on to Perth in Australia and by 1903 the station was fully operational, making these tiny and remote islands an essential link in the chain of communications by which Africa, Ceylon, Java, Singapore and the Australian continent were eventually able to maintain contact with the western hemisphere.

The staff of the cable station led a lonely life, as Direction Island, originally known as Rat Island or Pula Tikis to give it its native name, was only 1000 yards in length and 200 yards wide. In October 1910 a wireless unit was also installed and the station staff were able to keep in touch with passing ships.

The placid life of the islanders continued as it had for generations until in November 1914 His Imperial Majesty's German Ship *Emden* anchored off the islands and put a small landing party ashore on Direction Island to destroy the cable and wireless station. This was just three months after the world had been plunged into one of the bloodiest wars in history…

At the outbreak of World War 1, on 3rd August 1914, the German light cruiser *Emden*, commanded by Commander Karl von Muller of the Imperial German Navy, was cruising in the

Yellow Sea and approaching the Tsushima Straits between Japan and Russia as part of the German East Asia Squadron under Vice Admiral von Spee. When the Admiral decided to return with his squadron to Germany, Commander von Muller requested permission to remain in the East to carry out raids in the Indian Ocean. The *Emden* was affectionately known as 'The Swan of the East' because of her sleek appearance, but when permission was granted to detach from the rest of the squadron the ship was disguised by the addition of a dummy funnel.

Commander von Muller sailed his ship into the Pacific Ocean, down through the islands of the Dutch East Indies and into the Bay of Bengal. During the following three months she cruised around the coasts of India and Ceylon and as far west as the Chagos Archipelago before returning to the East Indies. During these first three months of the war the cruiser sank or captured 19 Allied ships and shelled several ports.

Commander von Muller kept two captured Allied supply ships near him, the *Buresk* and the *Exford*, which kept in constant touch with the cruiser, alleviating much of the worry that beset the captains of warships operating away from their base, particularly coal burning ships like the *Emden*, which consumed coal in vast quantities.

On leaving the Indies, it was von Muller's intention to sail to the Cocos Islands and destroy the cable and wireless station on Direction Island, so causing maximum disruption to Allied communications between the western and eastern hemispheres. His other objective was to deceive the Allied fleet into believing that he was moving south, back to the Pacific Ocean. He therefore signaled for the two supply ships to rendezvous with him at the islands and commenced what was to be the final 700-mile voyage of the 'Swan of the East'.

Arriving off Direction Island at 0600 hours on the morning of the 9th November 1914, the cruiser anchored in deep water and preparations were made to send a landing party ashore. While these preparations were being made, Mr Beauchamp, a member of the cable station's staff, came off the night watch and was returning to his quarters when he was informed that there was a strange ship lying off the island. He contacted Mr Farrant, the Station Superintendent and they climbed onto a roof where they could see an unidentified warship with four funnels. The vessel was not flying any flags and they agreed that one of the funnels appeared to be false. Mr Farrant returned to the wireless office and sent out an SOS message in plain language, informing anyone who was keeping a listening watch that there was a 'strange warship' off the islands; a message later changed to 'Emden here'.

Unbeknown to Commander von Muller, there was a large Allied convoy of troopships, heavily escorted by warships, passing in the vicinity of the islands and the message from the cable station operator was picked up by operators in the convoy. The convoy commander detached HMAS *Sydney*, commanded by Captain J.C.T. Glossop, to investigate the cause of the mysterious signals. The SOS and acknowledgement was also heard by the radio operator on the *Emden*, who wrongly estimated that the replying warship was at least 250 miles distance, about 10 hours sailing time. In actual fact the convoy was only 50 miles from the islands, a steaming time of only 2 hours.

Unaware of the true situation, Commander von Muller sent his landing party ashore under the command of his First Officer, Lieutenant Hellmuth von Mucke, a very capable and efficient Officer, with instructions to destroy the cable station and to sever the undersea cables, bringing back to the ship any confidential documents found. He then radioed for the supply ship *Buresk* to close in and replenish his diminishing supply of coal. No reply was received to this message but it did not cause any concern as it was assumed that the supply ship's radio may have been out of order. Preparations were made to 'coal ship' and when these were completed the ships crew relaxed on deck listening to the ship's band.

The *Buresk* was due to arrive at 0900 hours and shortly after this time the lookouts reported smoke to the north of the islands. The preparations to take on coal were resumed and at 0915 hours a further report was made that the approaching vessel appeared to have four funnels and two aerial encrusted masts. It soon became apparent that the approaching vessel was an enemy cruiser and it was known that any Allied cruiser in those waters carried heavier armament than the German ship.

A signal was hoisted and the ship's siren sounded, ordering the landing party to return to the ship immediately. Before they could do so, the cruiser slipped her anchor and with her huge battle ensign flying, steamed out to meet the threat of the approaching warship which opened fire with 15.2 cm guns, outgunning *Emden's* 10.5s. As the two ships drew closer the *Emden* was hit repeatedly and she was only then able to identify her opponent as HMAS *Sydney*.

The battle that followed was fought over some 30 square miles of sea and heavy damage was inflicted on both ships, with the heaviest being caused to the *Emden* although she did not sink.

With many dead and injured, Commander von Muller had little alternative but to beach the stricken cruiser on the reef off North Keeling Island, some 15 miles to the north of the main group of islands.

The surf on the reef was very heavy and few of the crew were able to get ashore, the rest having to stay on board, tending the injured and destroying valuable equipment which had not been damaged in the action and hoping to get off in due course without further loss of life.

With the *Emden* firmly stuck on the reef, HMAS *Sydney* broke off the action and immediately turned about to search for the *Buresk*. On sighting the supply ship, a shot was fired across her bows and she was ordered to heave to, whereupon her Captain immediately ordered her to be scuttled. Returning to the *Emden*, it was seen that the stricken cruiser had not struck her colours and, as Captain Glossops later reported, he reluctantly ordered a further broadside to be fired. Communications were finally established between the two ships and the *Sydney* signalled that she would be unable to attempt the rescue of survivors until a reconnaissance had been made of Direction Island the following morning.

The landing party under Lieutenant von Mucke, had arrived ashore on Direction Island shortly after 0630 hours. It comprised 3 Officers, 6 Petty Officers and 41 men who had been towed ashore by the *Emden's* steam cutter in two of the cruiser's cutters. Not knowing what sort of reception to expect and heavily armed with rifles, bayonets and pistols they hastily erected four heavy machine guns on suitable sites. Their orders were to destroy the wireless and cable stations and if possible to retrieve signal code and cypher books and any confidential documents found. From Direction Island three important cable links ran out into the ocean, providing Australia's only direct link with the United Kingdom. Other cables had already been cut by the German cruiser squadrons around the world.

Direction Island was some 3,000 metres from Port Refuge where the *Emden* had anchored. The island was quite small having a fairly level surface on which stood a few European bungalows, a radio tower and the cable station. Anchored near to the landing pier was a small white schooner bearing the name *Ayesha*, the name of a favourite wife of the Prophet Mohammed. A sailor was detailed to stand by the schooner with an explosive charge ready to sink her in due course.

The German party soon found the telegraph buildings and signal station, meeting no opposition. The Station Supervisor, Mr Farrant, was sent for and told that the station was to be destroyed and instructed to produce all confidential books and weapons. This was done and by a remarkable coincidence, Mr Farrant was able to inform Lieutenant von Mucke that a signal had recently been received from Reuters International News Agency, to the effect that the Kaiser had awarded the Lieutenant the Iron Cross for his part in previous actions.

The raiders set about demolishing the radio tower. The telegraph apparatus was smashed together with the radio transmitters, receivers and some of the furniture. All newspapers, books, morse cyphers etc. were collected and placed into bags ready for removal to the *Emden*. Two of the three undersea cables were located where they came ashore and were cut, the severed ends were towed out into the lagoon by the pinnace and dropped. Later reports indicated that the German raiders behaved well towards the cable station staff, who were civilians, and a spirit of camaraderie developed between the two groups.

As the demolition of the cable station proceeded, the *Emden's* siren was heard ordering a recall followed almost immediately by her huge signalling lamp ordering an immediate return to the ship. As the landing party re-embarked in the cutters they saw the *Emden* weigh anchor and commence to steam away. Following as best they could, they were amazed to see the huge battle flag unfurl and the cruiser loose off a broadside with her starboard guns. Then the sound of other gunfire was heard and they saw five columns of water shoot into the air astern of their ship. Realising that the cruiser was under fire from an as yet unseen warship, Lieutenant von Mucke ordered the small flotilla to return to the shore where he immediately established defensive positions and hoisted a German flag. The site was not good on such a low lying island but he was not prepared to give up the beachhead without a fight if it became necessary.

From their low-lying position on Direction Island, they were able to see little of the battle out at sea or determine who the enemy was. The thunder of the guns continued unabated and at one stage they saw the enemy ship but were unable to identify her. Both ships appeared to be damaged and the *Emden* had lost her forward funnel and was on fire aft. She looked to be in a poor condition and the outcome of the battle did not look good for the Germans.

As the battle drew further away and out of sight of those on the shore, Lieutenant von Mucke was faced with a dilemma. Should he stay in the hope that the *Emden* would return, or should he prepare a stronger defensive position in case the next ship to appear should be a British warship, in which case his small party could not hope to hold out against a superior force. Alternatively they could attempt to sail away and hope to evade the search parties that were bound to hunt for them.

A steam pinnace and two ships boats were not a very encouraging prospect when contemplating a voyage of over 600 miles to the nearest land. As he considered his choices, he remembered the schooner *Ayesha* and decided to give her a thorough inspection to determine her seaworthiness. She was undoubtedly old. For many years she had carried copra from the islands to the markets in Batavia two or three times each year, returning with stores for the islanders and the Clunies Ross estate. But as ships on regular freight routes had commenced to call at the islands, these trips had stopped and she had been left to rot in the lagoon.

On board the schooner was the captain, a Mr Partridge and two members of the Clunies Ross family, Edmund and Cosmo Clunies Ross (the latter was to die thirty years later as a prisoner of the Japanese in the infamous Changi Gaol at Singapore). All assured von Mucke that the boat was not seaworthy, but he was not convinced and made the decision to use her in a bid to escape from the islands.

As Lieutenant von Mucke's subsequent report to the German Naval Authorities shows, he was determined to try and extract his men from their predicament if humanly possible and take a chance in evading the Allied warships which were bound to search for them. When the Englishmen saw how determined the Germans were, they willingly gave their assistance, producing provisions, oil, blankets etc. They also gave advice as to the winds and currents in the area and forecast the weather that could be expected at that time of the year. Surprisingly the advice proved to be correct and although the two groups were now enemies, the preparations for an early departure by the Germans sailors went ahead in a spirit of *bonhomie*.

As dusk fell, the sails were hoisted and the German seamen hurried to get clear of the many coral outcrops and make a passage through the reef into the deep waters beyond, before it became fully dark. Thus, with the German ensign and battle flag flying, the schooner *Ayesha* became the newest Man o' War of His Imperial Majesty's German Navy!

The epic story of Lieutenant Hellmuth von Mucke and his small party of German sailors and their loyalty to their Emperor, Country and Service has been well documented. Suffice it to say that, having sailed from the Cocos Islands to the East Indies in an old and leaking boat, by superb seamanship, they then sailed back across the Indian Ocean to the Red Sea and then travelled by land across Arabia into Turkey, being involved in many fights on the way, they arrived in Constantinople on Whit Sunday, 23rd May 1915. There Lieutenant von Mucke and his small group, still in possession of the German flag which had first been erected on Direction Island, reported to Admiral Souchon, the Chief of the German Navy's Mediterranean Squadron using the time-honoured naval phrasing, " By your leave Sir, I beg to report the landing party from His Majesty's ship *Emden*, five Officers, seven Petty Officers and thirty-seven Seamen, reporting for duty".

For his fine act of leadership and devotion to duty, Lieutenant Hellmuth von Mucke was awarded the Iron Cross First Class and the rest of his men the Iron Cross Second Class.

The day following the battle off the Cocos Islands, HMAS *Sydney* returned to North Keeling Island and rescued the crew of the *Emden*. The wounded were treated and later the crew of a British gunboat, the *Cadmus*, had the terrible job of removing the dead from the hulk of the *Emden* for burial at sea. The *Emden* had been a ship of 3,650 tons, armed with ten 4-inch guns. 115 of her crew had been killed and 50 wounded, 4 more later died of wounds. Her opponent, HMAS *Sydney*, was of 5,400 tons and carried eight 6-inch guns. She suffered 4 men killed and 12 wounded.

On 16th November 1914, seven days after this epic battle, the cable ship *Patrol* arrived at Direction Island from Singapore and repaired the severed cable. The cable and wireless station was re-equipped with new apparatus and communications were soon re-established between the Eastern and Western hemispheres.

The remains of the once proud ship *Emden* remained firmly on the reef at North Keeling Island for four decades, gradually succumbing to the ravages of the sea and salt air until during the

1950s a Japanese salvage company removed much of the remains, leaving two rusty boilers on the shore and just a skeleton on the reef. Heavy seas have since swept away most of this. A few lucky visitors to the Cocos Islands may be in possession of small items of handicrafts that the islanders have made from pieces of the wreck.

At the time that the *Emden* was engaged in various actions in the Indian Ocean, Winston Churchill was the First Lord of the Admiralty. He later acknowledged that Commander Karl von Muller had fought his battles in a humane manner and in accordance with the International Laws of the sea, referring to him as 'one of the last gentlemen of War'.

Commander von Muller remained a prisoner of war until 1918 and the Kaiser awarded him Germany's highest honour, the 'Order Pour le Merite'. He died at the age of 50 years on 11th March 1923.

Since those dark days in World War 1 there have been three further ships in the German Navy to bear the name *Emden*. On 16th December 1916, a new light cruiser was commissioned and given the name *Emden*. After a short and active career she, along with other units of the German Navy, was scuttled at Scapa Flow under the terms of the armistice.

On the 7th January 1925, the first cruiser to be built in Germany after World War 1 was also named *Emden*, she made several world cruises and on her first voyage in 1926 visited the Cocos Islands to pay respect to the dead of 1914.

At various times the third *Emden* was under the command of Captain von Arnuald de la Periere, who had served on the original *Emden* in 1912 and also Captain Witthoeft who had been the Lieutenant in charge of the torpedo tubes during the epic battle of 1914. After a number of combat actions during World War II. She was finally severely damaged by bombs and beached near Kiel.

The name *Emden* was carried on by the Frigate F221 which was commissioned into the navy of the Federal Republic of Germany on 24th October 1961.

The naval action brought the Cocos/Keeling Islands briefly to the attention of peoples many miles distant but afterwards things soon returned to the tranquil life that had been known by generations of islanders.

John Sidney Clunies Ross, the fourth 'King of the Cocos Islands', assumed the mantle of his father and carried on putting into practice the ideas established by his kinsmen.

In October 1926 he married an English girl, a Miss Rose Nash, at the Church of St. Alban The Martyr, Fulham, a suburb of London. He brought his bride back to the islands and they duly had five children, their first being stillborn. Mrs Clunies Ross only stayed on the island for a few years before returning to England with the children. She did not return until 1947. In the twenty years between the two World Wars, the tranquility of life on the islands was only interrupted by the infrequent visits of trading vessels and the occasional sight of larger passenger ships which, because of their greater draught and the poor landing facilities, would anchor some miles out to sea.

Many of these liners were cruise ships of the P&O Line and Captain Brown of the liner SS *Morea* was the originator of the 'Cocos Barrel', a custom that survived for many years. In order to send a few luxuries ashore for the Cable Station staff on Direction Island and the islanders, a large barrel or cask would be filled with fresh meat, vegetables, magazines etc. and dropped over the ship's side for collection by the island's boats.

This action became known to the crews of other cruise ships plying between Ceylon and Australia and so the custom grew. On the 7th April 1939, RMS *Orien* was the last ship to 'drop the barrel' before the outbreak of World War II and in 1948 was the first ship to continue the tradition after the war.

On 13th Janaury 1950, the P&O liner *Strathaird* stopped off the islands and prepared to 'drop the barrel', but owing to the rough sea conditions was unable to do so. There were two 'dukons' (native craft) waiting nearby, in danger of being swamped; on one of them was John Clunies Ross, the 21-year-old 'King of the Cocos Islands'. The two crews were picked up by the liner and had to continue with them to Australia.

A small ship, the *Islander*, which was partly owned by the Clunies Ross Estates, called at the islands every three months and the annual visit of the District Officers from the Sraits Settlement made a welcome break in the islands routine.

In 1939, Captain P.G. Taylor of the Imperial Airways, carried out a trans-Indian Ocean flight between Kenya and Australia to assess the feasibility of using the Cocos Islands as a halfway or emergency stop for flying boats. He used a 'Guba' flying boat, the civil version of the Consolidated PBY which was later named the Catalina by the British. His survey showed that the area between Direction Island and Home Island was suitable for the landing of flying boats and the area was later marked and buoyed for this purpose.

A supply of aviation fuel was stored on the islands and the first aircraft to make use of these facilities were the flying boats of the Queensland and Northern Territories Air Service (QANTAS) and British Overseas Airways Corporation (BOAC), prior to the inauguration of a regular flying boat service between Ceylon and Australia and Africa and Australia.

In October 1940, HMS *Dandae* visited the islands at the request of the Ceylon Army Command to carry out a survey and to update the charts of the area (which had originally been made following Captain Fitzroy's visit in 1836 and were still in use).

When war did come to the Far East, the visits of the *Islander* ceased and the islands were kept supplied by naval vesssels which crept in under cover of darkness every three months with essential supplies.

Servicemen make their beds in the jungle during the construction of the Cocos Island air strip in 1945.

· Part II ·
1942 – 1946

Servicemen hard at work clearing the jungle during the construction of the Cocos Island air strip in 1945.

CHAPTER 5

A New Enemy

JAPAN'S AMBITION for an unchallenged leadership in the Far East began long before her successful campaign to oust the Dutch, British and Americans from their Colonial Empires in East Asia and the Pacific in 1941-2.

As far back as 1904, Japan's victory over Russia had awakened in the Japanese and other Asians the notion that Europeans were not invincible. In 1931 Japan had successfully invaded mainland China, occupying Manchuria and in 1937 had extended her control over Inner Mongolia and Northern China. Some of the main ports along the central and southern coasts of China were also seized and occupied.

In 1936, Japan had withdrawn from the London Naval Conference and within a year had broken the terms of the Washington Conference of 1921-22, which had fixed the tonnage of the capital ships of Great Britain, the United States and Japan, by considerably exceeding the naval programmes of France, Germany, Italy and Russia.

Japan continued to commit acts of aggression, particularly against China and, although the League of Nations and the Great Powers roundly condemned her, no positive action was taken, even when an American gunboat, the *Panay*, was bombed and sunk by Japanese war planes on 12th December 1937.

There can be little doubt that Japanese military leaders took this as a sign of weakness on the part of the Western Powers and with the developing crisis in Europe, took every opportunity to exploit it. When England and France were drawn into the conflict with Germany, Japan occupied the island of Haiman, which controlled the Gulf of Tonkin and in 1940, following the fall of France to the Germans, she moved troops into Indo China and forced Britain to cease supplying China via the Burma Road.

As Britain and her Allies became more embroiled with the war in Europe and America showed that she did not wish to become involved in armed conflict, Japan commenced to make preparations to extend her military forces throughout the Far East.

In January 1941, Admiral Yamamoto of the Imperial Japanese Navy, commenced to make a detailed study of the fortifications at Pearl Harbour on the island of Hawaii, which had become the new base for the American Pacific Fleet. He argued that unless the United States Navy in the Pacific Ocean was destroyed, Japan would have no hope of winning a war.

By the end of that month, Joseph Grew, the American Ambassador to Tokyo, was in possession of information showing the way that the Japanese military were thinking and he passed this information on to the State Department in Washington. Numerous other indications of the Japanese intentions in the Far East were received in Washington but the officials and politicians chose to ignore these warnings until in November 1941 it was finally accepted that a war with Japan was inevitable, by which time the die was cast.

On the 7th December 1941, a Japanese task force, which included aircraft carriers, arrived at a pre-determined position some 250 miles to the north of Hawaii. At 0600 hours the first two waves of 300 torpedo bombers, dive bombers and fighters commenced to take off from the decks of the carriers and set a course for Pearl Harbour, to carry out what was to be the most successful air raid of an as yet undeclared war, with the intention of destroying the American Pacific Fleet.

There was no warning that Sunday morning at 0730 hours when the attack commenced. Complete surprise was achieved and the results were spectacular. Three battleships were sunk among the many other vessels which were destroyed, together with two thirds of American naval aircraft. Many shore installations were damaged or destroyed and the American Army Air Force were left with only a very few undamaged aircraft on their airfields.

In this unprovoked attack on the American naval base, 2,403 Americans were killed and the Japanese had won a major victory for the loss of only 29 aircraft and 5 midget submarines. During the following four years Japan was to pay a very heavy price for her all too easy victory.

While the carrier-borne aircraft of the main Japanese fleet in Mid Pacific were having so much success at Pearl Harbour, other Japanese forces were simultaneously attacking Dutch, British and American possessions throughout the Far East.

On 10th December 1941, HMS *Prince of Wales* and HMS *Repulse* were attacked and sunk with heavy loss of life in the space of a few minutes by land-based aircraft of the Japanese XXII Air Flotilla. When the facts were known it became clear that senior naval officers ignored or had not learned the lessons gained from the fate of ships sailing close to land in the northern hemisphere without air support. The mission of these two ships and their escorts therefore had been suicidal from the time they sailed.

Hong Kong was attacked and after a brave but hopeless fight surrendered to Japanese forces on Christmas Day 1941. Malaya and Singapore were also invaded and by 15th February 1942 had also surrendered. The Japanese had complete success in the Dutch East Indies and occupied the islands of Java, Sumatra, Celebes and Timor. By 20th May 1942, the last British forces withdrew from Burma and crossed into India following the longest retreat in the history of the British Army.

In the Malayan campaign of 1942, the British, Indian and Australian forces lost a total of 138,708 troops of whom 130,000 were taken prisoner. In a campaign which had lasted for only 73 days and with a force that was only half the size of the Allies, the Japanese lost 3,507 dead and 6,150 wounded.

With hindsight, it is not difficult to lay the terrible consequences of the war in the Far East squarely on the shoulders of the pre-war politicians and the senior officers of the three services, who left our overseas forces ill-equipped, poorly trained and badly led.

Some of this stems from the government policies of 1935, when frantic measures were taken to increase our air forces at home but little was done in respect of the overseas commands. Neville Chamberlain became Prime Minister in 1937 and he and many of his Cabinet Ministers appeared to be under the misapprehension that Japan would not carry out any attacks unless Germany did.

At the time of the Japanese attacks, the Royal Air Force had less than 200 front line aircraft available in the whole of the Far East, these included a number of flying boat squadrons. The majority of the aircraft were obsolete and of little use in combat with more modern aircraft. Too late, these were re-enforced by a few Hawker Hurricanes.

As the short campaign developed, it soon became clear that many senior officers were out of touch with their forward troops and unaware just how bad the situation was, wherever the Japanese attacked. Probably due to the social structure within the forces at the time, they would take little heed of advice or opinions of those of junior rank, even when the latter were more *au fait* with conditions. This became very evident when senior officers of the army dealt with the Royal Air Force, particularly in the East Indies, where their ignorance of the limitations or otherwise of aircraft became apparent.

It is not the intention of this book to dwell on the mistakes and failings of the military and political leaders of those far off days, merely to set the scene which eventually led to some 7,000 men of the three services being sent over 1,000 miles from the nearest Allied base to some remote islands in the Indian Ocean and there to construct and operate a Royal Air Force bomber base and Air Staging Post in the latter days of the war against Japan.

It was Japan's declared political objective to set up a Greater East Asia Co-Prosperity Sphere, to be dominated by herself and comprising the Philippine Islands, the Netherlands East Indies and Malaya. Burma was to be occupied for strategic purposes and also as a source of vital supplies, especially oil and rice. Apparently Japan had no designs on the mainland of the United States or Great Britain, her objectives being confined to the Far East.

By early 1942, with many British and Allied ships sunk or put out of action in Far Eastern waters, the Japanese Fleet was able to roam almost at will over the Indian Ocean, going as far West as the Arabian Sea and down the East coast of Africa, where they inflicted many casualties on Allied ships and men.

The Japanese land forces came no further West than the Dutch East Indies, other than to seize Christmas Island, which is 550 miles to the East of the Cocos Islands.

This tiny island was garrisoned by a small unit of the Hong Kong and Singapore Coastal Artillery which comprised 28 Other Ranks, 4 NCOs and a British Officer. On the 4th March 1942, ships of the Japanese Navy appeared off the island and commenced a bombardment. There was little hope of relief for the small force and they had no option but to hoist the white flag of surrender. Before the Japanese forces landed, the Indian soldiers of the defence force murdered their officer and the 4 NCOs, presumably in the hope of gaining favour with their conquerors.

When the war with Japan was over the men of the Christmas Island garrison were traced to Java, where they were arrested and taken to Singapore for trial. Of the seven men who were tried, one was sentenced to death by hanging and the others were given long prison sentences. Two years later an eighth man was traced, arrested, and tried. He was convicted and also sentenced to death but both of the death sentences were commuted to that of life imprisonment.

Only 550 miles to the West of Christmas Island were the Cocos Islands, strategically important because of the cable station, which, unknown to the Japanese, was to remain open throughout the war, maintaining the vital and only link of it's kind between Australia and the rest of the world.

The cable link to the West was to Rodrigues, Mauritius and then on to Durban, South Africa, the one to the East went to

Batavia, Java and on to Singapore. This link was sealed off for the duration of the war. Two more cables connected with Freemantle, Australia. So remote and small, the islands were indefensible against any but the lightest of attacks.

AA gun emplacement, Cocos Islands, 1944.

CHAPTER 6

War Returns to the Islands

IN 1940 THE AUSTRALIANS installed a high frequency direction finding (HF/DF) wireless station on Direction Island and in 1941 Ceylon Army Command provided a platoon of Indian Infantry together with two very old 6-inch naval guns which were sited on Horsburgh Island to cover the entrance to the area known as Port Refuge and avoid a repetition of the *Emden* incident of 1914 when the enemy ship was able to anchor off the entrance to the lagoon unchallenged. The guns were manned by Sinhalese gunners of the 1st Coastal Regiment of the Ceylon Coastal Artillery under the command of a British Officer.

In 1941 HMS *Danae* put a survey party ashore on North Keeling Island and discovered a hidden cache of 700 barrels of diesel oil and 400 drums of Japanese submarine fuel.

Why the Japanese did not occupy the Cocos Islands is not known, perhaps they had come to the conclusion that the islands were too difficult to defend. They must have been aware that there was a cable station on Direction Island, however, and yet they made no serious attempt to destroy it; nothing more than a few aerial reconnaissance flights, some indiscriminant bombing and a few shells fired from out at sea.

On the 5th February 1942 the buildings on Direction Island which housed the Cable Station and staff quarters was the subject of shelling from the sea. No vessel was seen and it was assumed that a submarine was responsible. Only slight damage was caused and there were no casualties.

On 13th February 1942 the operators on Direction Island received a final sad message from their colleagues at the Singapore end of the cable link. It stated, "So long chaps, this is goodbye". The link was sealed off and no further messages were passed for over 3½ years.

Nearly a month later, on 3rd March 1942, the Cable Station was again the subject of shelling. During this raid a Chinese Carpenter was killed. By this time large decoy fires had been prepared, these were lit in the hope that the Japanese would be deceived into believing that they had been successful in destroying the Station. The Japanese radio later reported that many fires had been seen and the Cable Station had been destroyed. This may have been because, with the consent of the Admiralty, a wireless message was sent in plain language to the Cable Station in Batavia advising them to disconnect their cable instruments as those on Direction Island had been permanently knocked out. The deception was maintained by painting shell holes on the roofs of the buildings.

The occasional flying boat continued to land on the lagoon and in March 1942 a Dutch-manned Catalina landed and struck an underwater coral head, which tore a large hole in it's hull. A group of islanders hauled the machine out of the water, patched the hole and the aircraft was airborne within a few hours.

It was during 1942 that the War Cabinet Chiefs of Staff became concerned with the vulnerability of British bases in the Indian Ocean and called for reports on the action that would be required to defend them.

Among the papers that were subsequently submitted was one in respect of the Cocos Islands. The report was based on the importance of the islands as an essential cable relay station in the Allied lines of communications between London and Australia. The report suggested that it was unlikely that the islands would be used as a base for operational flying boats although they already had limited facilities which were used by BOAC and QANTAS in emergencies. The report also pointed out that the islands were quite indefensible against a large scale attack.

A number of recommendations were made including the suggestion that 8 heavy and 12 light anti aircraft guns should be sited on Direction Island and an additional Radio Direction Finding (RDF), Station be constructed, to include a 180' high tower which would give extended all round advanced notice of approaching vessels and aircraft. Other recommendations were that consideration be given to the laying of a minefield between Direction and Horsburgh Islands and that the existing garrison be increased to a force of sufficient size to offer a delay to any attempt at invasion until reinforcements could be sent.

The Officer submitting the report attached an addendum, recommending that it be forwarded to General Wavell, the Commander-in-Chief, India, with instructions to take immediate steps to implement the recommendations to reinforce the existing garrison on the islands, to stop them becoming another Wake Island.

This was a reference to an action by a small force of American troops, which earned them the admiration of the World, for their spirited defence of the small island of Wake in the Pacific Ocean against a large Japanese invasion force and who may have been saved had nearby American carrier borne aircraft been permitted to attack the invading forces while they were being disembarked from their transports.

The Vice Chief of the Air Staff also added a rider, that General Wavell should be made aware of the strategic importance of the islands as a potential base for reconnaissance aircraft employed in the Indian Ocean and of their importance as a staging post on the alternative air route to Australia. None of these suggestions appear to have been implemented at the time.

While these matters were under discussion in London, a signal was received that there had been a mutiny among some of the Singhalese troops on the Cocos Islands and an attempt had been made to murder the British officer in charge of the garrison artillery. A warship was immediately sent with orders to quell the mutiny and arrest the ringleaders, the chief of whom appeared to be a Bombardier of the Coast Artillery.

The background to the mutiny is easy to understand. Since 1941, the Asian people had seen the Japanese forces over-run Hong Kong, Malaya, Burma, the East Indies and many islands in the Pacific Ocean, breaking the rule of white supremacy and showing that the white races were not invincible to the Eastern races who were in every respect superior.

The Japanese fleet had crossed the Indian Ocean almost unopposed, shelling Colombo and Trincomalee in Ceylon, while the Royal Navy prepared to withdraw to the sanctuary of the East African coast. Northern India awaited invasion, as did Australia where there had been a number of air raids. The Cocos Islands, hitherto a backwater of the war, was now projected into the front line.

Part of the small Cocos Island garrison was the 11th Battery of the 1st Ceylon Coastal Artillery, which was composed entirely of Singhalese men commanded by a British Officer. The garrison was made up of 55 Artillerymen, 5 Ceylonese Engineers, 36 Infantrymen, 1 member of the Ceylon ARC and 2 Medical Orderlies.

With the Allies being beaten in every direction it could have been expected that some of the poorly educated young soldiers recruited into the armed forces of the Commonwealth should become confused as to where their loyalties lay.

The Artillerymen had been part of the first contingent to volunteer for duty overseas and some had already seen service on the Seychelles Islands where they later alleged that German prisoners of war appeared to be treated better than coloured soldiers in the Commonwealth forces.

On reaching Island 'X', the Army code name for the Cocos Islands, they found that a British Officer had been appointed over Singhalese and Burghers (Anglo Indians). This fanned their anti-Colonial feelings although they had not shown any signs of restlessness or dissatisfaction at their posting to a remote group of islands in what had now become a Japanese lake.

Bombardier G.H. Fernando, of the 1st Ceylon Coastal Artillery, volunteered for overseas duty following a broken love affair and other setbacks while in Ceylon. At one time he had lived in

Kelantan, Malaya, where he had become incensed at the way in which white people treated the coloured population. He was a firm believer in Asia for the Asians and when he saw how the Japanese had over-run so many lands formerly run by white men he thought that perhaps his dream was about to come true. It would appear that Fernando was more anti-European than anti-British.

It was this man's political beliefs which were the mainspring of the mutiny, which he planned as a means of delivering the islands to the Japanese in the hope that it would further the cause of Asian unity. At one time he had thought of stealing the islanders boats and sailing them to Christmas Island, the nearest Japanese controlled territory.

Over a period of weeks he tried to interest some of his subordinates in his ideas but without any success. Undaunted, he formulated a plan to disarm the small guard on the gun site and to kill the white Officer in the belief that if this was done the small contingent of infantry who were stationed on Direction Island could be persuaded to kill their own Officer and join him or they too would be killed. When this had been accomplished, the cable station would be destroyed and he would find a means of contacting the Japanese.

Following the bombardments in February and March, he increased his efforts to recruit others to his way of thinking and during the month preceding the mutiny he succeeded in convincing ten other Artillerymen to join in with his scheme as to him it was obvious that the Cocos Islands were due to be conquered by the Japanese.

On the 8th May 1942, Bombardier Fernando was the NCO in charge of the guard on the gun site. With his fellow mutineers around him, he and two others locked up the remaining guards in their quarters and broke into the armoury. He armed himself with a tommy-gun but was unable to locate the magazine so swapped it for a Bren gun. All had not gone smoothly however; some of the men who should have been asleep were awake and created sufficient noise to awaken their Officer, Lieutenant Henry

Stephens. He went to the gun site and as he approached one of the mutineers fired at him and wounded him. The mutineers positioned themselves in the gun emplacements and for over two hours kept up a spasmodic fire directed mostly towards the main living quarters where the remainder of the detachment were quartered.

During the confusion, Lieutenant Stephens gathered together 21 loyal men of the unit and they kept up a steady rate of fire against the mutineers, wounding one and causing another to run away. One of the Lieutenant's men, Gunner Samual Jayasekera was killed.

It soon became apparent to the confused and misguided men who had aligned themselves with Bombardier Fernando, that they had little chance of successfully accomplishing their plan. They held a conference and when called upon to surrender they did so. Arrested and disarmed a Court Martial was held under the Garrison Commander, Captain George Gardiner, and seven of the mutineers were sentenced to death by shooting.

When a report of the action and trial was sent to Ceylon Army Command, it was not accepted and the Garrison Commander was instructed to send the prisoners to Colombo, where they would be tried by a properly conveyed Court Martial.

At his trial, the Bombardier made a plea in mitigation of his actions, stating that they were as a result of his resentment at the treatment of coloured people by their white rulers, which had been fermenting in his mind for years and also that, being a member of the armed forces, he felt the war in which he was involved was detrimental to the interests of the Asian people.

However, the men on trial were unable to dispute the overwhelming evidence that the prosecution was able to submit and they were all convicted and sentenced to death by hanging. Following their convictions in the Supreme Court in Colombo, they were returned to the prison to await confirmation of their sentences by the Viceroy.

A few days later it was confirmed that three of the men were to hang, the others had their sentences commuted to long terms of imprisonment.

Bombardier G.H. Fernando, as ringleader of the ill fated mutiny, was one of those who had his sentence confirmed and he was subsequently hanged in Colombo jail on the 5th July 1942. The other two sentenced to death were Gunner G.B. De Silver and Gunner C.A. Gauder. One of them had shot and wounded his Commanding Officer in an attempt at murder and the other had shot and killed a fellow Gunner. They were hanged two days later. Gunner C.A. Gauder was executed on his 21st birthday.

During the six years of the Second World War, there were only four executions for military offences in the British Army, three of these being the men involved in the mutiny on the Cocos Islands in 1942. During the same period there were thirty-six military executions for murder.

Following the Japanese occupation of Singapore and the Straits Settlements, an Order in Council was signed at Buckingham Palace on 1st July 1942 by H.M. King George V1, in which power was given to the Governor of Ceylon to apply Defence Regulations, which had previously been enforced by the Governor of Singapore, on various communities, including the Cocos Islands, until such time as they could be restored back to him.

In 1943, the Royal Australian Air Force established a meteorological unit on Direction Island and strengthened the existing HF/DF section. A Naval 'Y' section was already in operation and its strength was also increased. This section was staffed by highly trained telegraphists who intercepted Japanese wireless signals, passing them to Allied code and cypher experts for decoding.

The Australian airline QANTAS commenced to operate two Catalina flying boats per week between Ceylon and Australia on behalf of BOAC. This service was later increased to five and had a flight time of 28 hours, but the Cocos Islands were only used as an emergency refuelling stop when necessary.

The newly formed Royal Air Force Transport Command also expressed an interest in using the islands and provided two additional Catalinas from their United Kingdom and West Africa route.

After the fall of Singapore, Pan American Airways made strenuous efforts to obtain the permission. of the Australian Government to operate on this route and General Birkell, the Officer Commanding the 10th United States Air Force in India, offered to supply two Clippers using the Cocos Islands as a base.

The Commander-in-Chief of the British Eastern Fleet sent an urgent signal to the Admiralty asking them to persuade the Americans not to press for this, as the Japanese appeared to be unaware that the cable link to Australia was still in operation. Should they become aware of increased air activity in the vicinity of the islands, they could well attack and destroy this vital link in Allied communications.

Although internationally known, the Cocos Islands became the top secret islands of the Indian Ocean. They were never referred to by name in official communications but were always given a code name, of which there were several. The islands were even deleted from maps and charts showing the disposition of Allied troops in the hope that should any of these fall into Japanese hands the omission of the islands would not be noticed. It is impossible to assess how successful these deceptions were, but the islands were never subjected to any serious attack.

CHAPTER 7

The Dawn of a New Era

A BIG STEP leading to a change in the fortunes of the Allies in the Far Eastern theatre of operations, was the creation in 1943 of the South East Asia Command (SEAC) with Lord Louis Mountbatten as the Supreme Commander.

The defeat of the Axis powers in the West was the first priority of the Allies but, even at this early stage, the planners were aware that when this was accomplished a large part of Bomber Command and the United States Air Forces in Europe would need to be transferred to the Pacific theatre of war in order to achieve the defeat of Japan, as well as thousands men and tons of war materials.

These Air Forces, later to be designated 'Tiger Force', would need to be transferred via a chain of Air Staging Posts over the thousands of miles between Europe and the East, whichever route was taken to reach the Pacific.

The Supreme Commander issued instructions to the Chief of Staff (Plans) to arrange for Royal Air Force and Army Engineering Officers to survey various locations throughout South East Asia Command with a view to establishing such Staging Posts as necessary. Among the many sites considered was the Cocos Islands.

Arrangement were made for a survey team to visit the islands to determine the feasibility of establishing an Air Staging Post capable of receiving multi-engined aircraft *en route* from Ceylon to Australia and the creation of a heavy bomber base.

In February 1944, a survey team was assembled and sailed for the islands under the command of Commander E.E. Coombe, RN. The team used Admiralty chart No. 2510 of the Cocos/Keeling islands which had originally been compiled by Captain Robert Fitzroy, RN in 1836, being updated in 1860, 1865 and 1891.

The findings of the survey were based mainly on a report submitted by Major J.D.A. Charteries of the Royal Engineers, which indicated that West Island, the largest in the main group, could be suitably developed by a Forward Airfield Construction Group in a relatively short period of time.

The report suggested that a 2½ mile length of road could be constructed from a possible bridgehead to the commencement of a runway within three to four days. Given suitable equipment, three runways, dispersals, hardstandings etc could be completed within 60 days at the following rate:

D + 7. One strip 1000 yds x 50 yds plus an apron 300 yds x 50 yds capable of operating two squadrons of fighters.

D + 17 A medium bomber strip of 1600 yds x 50 yds, two fighter aprons 300 yds x 50 yds for two fighter squadrons and one medium bomber squadron.

D + 40 One heavy bomber strip 2000 yds x 50 yds.

D + 60 A total of three heavy bomber strips each 2000 yds x 50 yds, four fighter aprons 300 yds x 50 yds, two dispersals loops 5000 yds x 50 yds and one hundred hardstandings for four fighter squadrons, two medium bomber squadrons and two heavy bomber squadrons.

Included with the report were detailed plans showing the disposition of the proposed runways, aprons and taxi tracks.

The findings of the survey team were passed to the Supreme Commander, who directed that a planning committee be formed from members of all three Services, with a view to developing the suggestions put forward.

The War Planning Staff in SEAC were at that time formulating plans for the recapture of Malaya and the islands of the Dutch East Indies – operations 'Zipper' and 'Mailfist'. By July of 1944 they submitted a report showing the operating potentials of the Cocos Islands if they were developed into a Royal Air Force base. The report showed the possible operational use of the base as;

(1) An intermediate Staging Post between Ceylon and Australia for aircraft and surface vessels of limited range.

(2) An advanced airfield for mounting photographic recon-naissance, covering areas of the East Indies which are at present out of P.R.range.

(3) An advanced airfield for use by up to four squadrons of bombers plus a permanent fighter defence.

(4) Increased radio facilities, including equipment for the Naval 'Y' Service.

(5) As a base for air/sea rescue when operations required them.

(6) As a minor advanced base for operations against Java and South Sumatra.

(7) Feign and deception may enable us to tie down Japanese forces in the Sumatra/Java areas. By using pierced steel plating (psp) on a bed of rolled coral, the base could be operational within fourteen days.

By 1944 the war situation was changing, both in Europe and the Far East. In London the Air Ministry planners were also looking ahead to when hostilities ceased in Europe and a massive influx of aircraft and war materials would need to be transferred to the Far East and ultimately Australia should that country become the main base for activities in the South Pacific.

The Air Staff were also studying the various air routes to Australia. Principally the routes were;

(a) Via the Middle East-India-Ceylon-Cocos Islands.

(b)   Via the North Atlantic-North America-North Pacific.

(c)   Via the North Atlantic-Azores-Bermuda-Nassau-British Honduras-South Pacific.

It was found that the route via the Cocos Islands was 3,000 miles shorter from the United Kingdom and 5,550 miles shorter from the Middle East than any of the other routes examined. From the United Kingdom to Australia via the Cocos Islands, the distance was 11,000 miles while the shortest of the other routes was 14,000 miles.

The conclusions arrived at by the Air Staff were that, unless a Pacific strategy was definitely ruled out, the Joint Planning Staff were to undertake an urgent and thorough investigation as to the suitability of the Cocos Islands being developed into an Air Staging Post and to ensure an adequate defence. It was at this stage that the Chief of Air Staff in London was made aware that the Planning Staff in South East Asia Command had been working on similar plans and that Lord Louis Mountbatten, the Supreme Commander, was even then en-route to London with the findings and recommendations of his own planning team.

On arriving in London, Admiral Mountbatten passed his reports to the War Cabinet who found them to be of a similar nature to the conclusions arrived at by the Chief of Air Staff and his planners.

In August 1944, the decision was taken by the British and American Joint Chiefs of Staff to develop the Cocos Islands as a matter of urgency, into an Air Staging Post with an adequate fighter defence, subject to a further survey.

At the time that these plans were being discussed there were an estimated 80,000 Japanese troops of all arms on Sumatra, supported by 110 aircraft in the northern part and 50 in the south. These consisted of 50 fighters in both north and south and 30 medium bombers and 30 torpedo bombers in the north. The primary task of the fighters in the south was to defend the oil refineries at Palembang.

Both during and after their conquest of the Dutch East Indies, single Japanese aircraft had made a number of sorties over the Cocos Islands, using both Naval and Army planes. These had occurred on 1st, 10th,16th and 24th December 1943 and on 3rd and 13th January 1944. No bombs were dropped on any of these occasions and the height of the aircraft varied from 10,000 feet down to just above the treetops.

The Australian airline QANTAS were using five Catalina flying boats on the Ceylon to Australia route and often the aircraft landed on the lagoon at the Cocos Islands. On 14th February 1944, one of their Catalina's was at its mooring when a Japanese reconnaissance aircraft flew overhead. On sighting the flying boat it dropped one bomb which missed it's target. Further reconnaissance flights were made on 14th, 16th, and 18th March; 14th April, 30th June, and 10th July 1944. On none of these occasions were any bombs dropped.

On the 8th August 1944, a Japanese 'Sally' aircraft appeared over the islands at a height of 10,000 feet. After circling a few times, it dropped a number of bombs and then came down to just above treetop height where it carried out machine gun attacks on all three of the inhabited islands. During the attacks a Naval Rating and three civilians were killed and three other Servicemen were injured. A number of fires were started and 27 native houses were damaged or destroyed. Fearing further attacks, the islanders scattered throughout the islands for a short time.

A few days after the attack by the Japanese aircraft, John Sidney Clunies Ross, the fourth 'King of the Cocos Islands', died from natural causes at the age of 75 years. He was the great-grandson of Clunies Ross Primus and at the time of his death, 117 years after his kin had settled on the islands, it was estimated that he had only one part Scots blood in his veins and seven parts Malayan. He was buried in the Clunies Ross family plot.

The heir to the Clunies Ross estate, John Cecil Clunies Ross, was a young man of 16 years, at the time of his father's death and was in England with his mother Rose and two younger brothers. He was attending college to study estate management and the

Malayan language and customs. He was unable to return to the islands until 1947 when he found that the native population for whom he was responsible had increased to 1,556.

When news of the death of Clunies Ross was received, the Commander-in-Chief, Ceylon Army Command, sent Major, later Lieutenant Colonel, Jessaming of the Indian Army Ordinance Corps to the islands as the Military Advisor. This was done with the approval of the Governor of Ceylon, the Cocos Islands being under his jurisdiction for the duration of the war or until the Straits Settlement was free from Japanese occupation. On the 9th September 1944, a further air attack was made on the islands when a Japanese twin-engined bomber dropped bombs and then flew low, firing its machine guns. No damage was caused in this attack and on 27th October 1944 another twin-engined enemy aircraft appeared over the islands, circled a few times and then flew away.

At the time of these air attacks there was only a token military force on the islands under the command of a Major May, a Royal Marines Officer who was designated Fortress Commander. The title was somewhat of a misnomer, giving the impression of a large command when in fact it consisted of one platoon of Royal Marines under an Officer with a Sergeant and 28 men on Home Island, two platoons on Direction Island, a small headquarters company, a detachment of East African troops of No. 22 East Africa Brigade under an Officer and a section of the Ceylon Coastal Artillery.

There was also a small naval contingent operating the HF/DF station and 'Y' Service and a Royal Australian Air Force Meteorological section. In all a total of about 200 men.

CHAPTER 8

'Operation Pharos'

THE COMMANDER-IN-CHIEF Allied Land Forces South East Asia informed the War Cabinet that owing to forthcoming land operations in Burma and Malaya, he was unable to supply the men and materials that would be needed to develop the Cocos Islands. The Air Ministry therefore agreed to fly out from the United Kingdom various Officers, who on arrival in India would report to Air Command South East Asia (Plans) in Delhi, where they would constitute the Royal Air Force Planning Team. The Air Ministry also agreed to supply the greater part of the Royal Air Force personnel who would be required to staff the proposed air base.

The Supreme Commander instructed that a joint operation be prepared for the construction of and operating of a Royal Air Force Station and Air Staging Post on the Cocos Islands. The proposed project was given the code name 'Operation Pharos'. The code names given to wartime operations had no significant meaning or bearing on the actual operations and were merely a means of concealing the identity or location of various projects and was a reference point when the matter was under discussion. Were there scholars among the planners who were aware that 'Pharos' was the Roman word for lighthouse and that in 248 BC, a lighthouse, which was to become one of the Seven Wonders of the World, was built on the island of Pharos, off the port of Alexandria, Egypt?

The Royal Air Force team was to be under the control of a dynamic Australian, Group Captain, later Air Commodore, A.W.

Hunt, who was the current Deputy Director of Plans (Air) at ACSEA. His Staff Officer with the Force Planners was to be Wing Commander R.M. Mason, who was also with ACSEA Plans.

The Convent of St Bridget's in Colombo, Ceylon, was taken over as the headquarters for the planning team and meetings commenced.

The first meeting of the Joint Planning Staff was held on the 7th December 1944. At the commencement of the meeting, Flight Lieutenant Saunders of 222 Group, the Force Security Officer, reported that even at that early stage information had already been leaked that some special task was being considered. As a result he had arranged that all telephone calls at Air Headquarters would be monitored.

All three of the armed services were involved in the planning of the operation and the committee members consisted of;

PLANNING STAFF (ARMY)	PLANNING STAFF (RAF)
Ceylon Army Command	Fortress Commander (Designate).
AA.QMG.(Lt.Col)	Administration Officer.
A.L.F.S.E.A.(Rep.)	Senior Equipment Officer.
C.R.E.	Senior Engineering Officer.
R.E.(Airfields).	Senior Signals Officer.
R.E.(Petrol).	Senior Radar Officer.
DAA.QMG.from ALFSEA.	Senior Medical Officer.
D.A.D.S.J.	Senior Movements Officer.
Royal Navy(Rep).	Force Security Officer.
Office of Works & Water.	Adjutant.

At the first meeting it was decided that each of the departments involved in the operation would submit plans covering the needs and requirements of the units that they were responsible for. It was recommended that two reconnaissance parties should visit the islands and carry out a further survey in preparation for the action that would need to be taken.

On 10th December 1944, the Headquarters of Air Command, South East Asia, issued Formation Order No. 308 for the formation of No. 129 Air Staging Post ex-United Kingdom, with an effective date of the formation being the 8th December 1944. On 3rd January 1945, Formation Order No. 332 was issued for the formation of Royal Air Force Station 'Brown' at RAF Station Kalyan, India, which was to be the main assembly point for the RAF personnel who would be manning the new station. At this stage 'Brown' was the code name given to the as yet undeveloped RAF base on the Cocos Islands until security should permit otherwise.

The first of the two survey parties assembled at RAF Station, Koggala, Ceylon, on 10th December 1944, where they boarded Catalina flying boat 'L' of No. 205 Squadron for the flight to the Cocos Islands. The members of this party were:

Group Captain A.W. Hunt – Fortress Commander (Des)

Colonel Smyster USAF – Rep of Eng-in- Chief SACSEA.

Lt.Col. J.C.Simpson – AQMG, ALFSEA (Plans).

Major P.E. Holmes – Dep/Dir/Mov, Ceylon Army.

Major J.F. Hedges – Royal Signals.

Brig. R.H. Duckworth, OBE, MC
Chief Engineer, Ceylon Army Command.

The aircraft was piloted by the Squadron's Commanding Officer, Wing Commander MacMillan, with Flight Lieutenant Lowden as his second pilot. This was the first visit that either pilot had made to the Cocos Islands and after a long, but uneventful flight of 13 hours 20 minutes they spent a further 27 minutes checking the landing area for hidden coral heads and flotsam, always a source of worry to flying-boat pilots. On becoming waterborne the aircraft made a run of 15-18,000 yards before finally anchored in the lagoon where they were met by the Manager of the Cable Station from Direction Island who arranged for the aircraft to be refuelled from 4-gallon tins of petrol by native labour – a long, hot and laborious chore. Army personnel of the small garrison arranged food and tented accommodation for the passengers while the aircrew prepared for the return flight. During the time that the Catalina was on the water, part of the tail section was damaged by the mast of the Cable Station Manager's boat, however this was repaired and the crew made a successful take-off at 1700 hours for another all-night flight. All aircraft flights to the Cocos Islands were made during darkness until the airfield became operational and had an adequate fighter defence, the aircraft arriving shortly after dawn.

Two days later, Flight Lieutenant Escott of No. 205 Squadron flew the second survey group to the islands in Catalina 'S'. This party comprised:

Lt Col A.M. Shaw – ADH & PHQ Ceylon Army;

Cdr Chaplin – Royal Navy;

Cpt Thompson – Tank & Marine Expert;

Sq/Ldr Davidson – Radar Plans (ACSEA).

Following these two initial flights, aircraft of No. 205 Squadron flew to the Cocos Islands several times a week during the whole period of 'Operation Pharos' and beyond, transporting freight, mail and personnel on both inward and outward journeys. During one of the early visits an aircraft from the squadron made a photographic record of the islands and the landing area in the lagoon. Throughout the war, the squadron's Catalinas and later the giant four-engined Sunderland flying boats, had the additional task of ferrying mail and personnel on the Ceylon to Australia route.

Harold Daly, a pilot with the squadron, remembers being briefed on 3rd January 1945 to take two Army Surveyors to 'Brown', a location that he had never heard of. This was one of the many code names given to the Cocos Islands in an endeavour to confuse the enemy. Security must have been good because it was several weeks before he heard that a Royal Air Force base was being constructed on the islands.

Taking off from his base at Koggala, Ceylon in the early evening, his navigator plotted a course by dead reckoning, there being no navigational aids on the islands, so as to arrive shortly after dawn. The night flights were essential in order to avoid interception by the Japanese and also so as not to draw attention to increased air activity in the vicinity of the islands.

The flight of more than 1,700 miles over the featureless Indian Ocean lasted a long and tedious 14 hours 20 minutes before landing on the lagoon and tying up at a buoy off Direction Island ready to be re-fuelled for the return flight later that day. The crew were ferried ashore in native boats and given a meal by Army personnel. To men who were used to the swarming crowds of India and Ceylon, the islands appeared to be an idyllic place to stay although, with each island densely covered with swaying coconut palms there was no way they could have visualised that in a few weeks there would be a fully operational RAF air base operating heavy bombers and reconnaissance aircraft with a fighter defence squadron situated on one of the islands.

Among the many experts who visited the islands on subsequent flights, were some who had gained their experience in the construction of coral based airstrips on Addu Atoll in the Maldive Islands, some 600 miles to the west of Ceylon. Others would use their expertise in port construction, the installation of petrol and oil facilities, the building of jetties to assist in the unloading of waterborne stores and many other matters where expert knowledge was required.

Following many meetings of the Planning Staff, the names of the Senior Officers of the new base were announced. These were:

Fortress Commander	Group Captain A.W. Hunt
Naval Officer in Charge	Captain Stalk, R.N.
Senior Army Officer	Lt Col Hardy, RASC.
Civil Affairs Officer	Lt Col Hartley, M.A.

Chief Engineer	Lt Col Brown, R.E.
RAF Station Commander	Wg Cdr Macpherson, RAF
O/C No. 129 Air Staging Post	Wing Commander Butcher, RAF

The Admiral in Charge of the East Indies Fleet was to assume responsibility for the marking of all channels and anchorages and to make available a number of freighters and tankers for the operation.

The first setback occurred when HMS *Hirm* found that the tides were 2ft 2ins lower than had first been reported and that owing to the growth of coral outcrops, only ships with a draught of 15ft or less would be able to use the main western channel into the lagoon instead of those with a 21ft draught that had been earmarked to take part in the operation. The plans for the invasion of Malaya, Operation Zipper, were well advanced and because of this forthcoming operation, ships of a shallower draught were at a premium.

Eventually some ships of 1,350 and 1,700 tons were located but larger vessels would be required to anchor some 4 to 5 miles out at sea and have their cargo ferried ashore by lighters and landing craft.

The Ceylon Army Command undertook to supply all the Army units and their equipment, together with landing craft and their crews to ferry men and equipment ashore on the northern tip of West Island, which was the island on which the airfield was to be built.

Owing to the tide movements, this work would be limited to four hours per day during daylight hours. The heaviest pieces of equipment to be unloaded from the ships would be the crated Spitfire fuselages, each weighing 3 tons 3 cwt and were 26ft x 5ft 8in x 6ft 8in in size, an 18-ton Lorraine crane, 15-ton caterpillar tractors and other heavy plant such as bulldozers, graders, scrapers, dumpers, excavators, trenchers, rooters, etc. All these machines would be required by the Engineer, Pioneer and Artisan

Companies who would have the heaviest and hardest work to do once ashore.

By January 1945, the Royal Marine detachment on the Cocos Islands were long overdue for relief. When they received orders to move, their place was taken by a half battery of the 17th Indian Light Anti-Aircraft Regiment who dispersed their 40 mm guns on Home and Direction Islands. The stay of this unit was a short one, as a few weeks later they were to be relieved by No. 2962 Squadron of the Royal Air Force Regiment, a unit that had been formed especially to take part in Operation Pharos.

During their time on the islands, the Indian AA Unit tracked a Catalina flying boat of QANTAS Airways which arrived unann-ounced and landed on the lagoon to carry out repairs.

The arrival of this aircraft proved a bonus for the unit's Commanding Officer, as when the aircraft was air tested, the Captain permitted him to be aboard and he was able to see at first-hand how efficient his men had been at camouflaging their guns.

Early in February 1945, Lieutenant Colonel J.E.B. Jessimine, who had become the Islands Military Adviser on the death of John Sydney Clunies Ross in August 1944, became time expired and was replaced by Commander G.M.L. Williams, RNVR. At the same time, Lieutenant Colonel Harvey, M.A. became the Islands Civil Affairs Officer.

With approval having been given for the development of the Cocos Islands into an Air Staging Post and RAF bomber base, the tremendous task of selecting and bringing together all the units, men, equipment and ships that would be required for the successful accomplishment of 'Operation Pharos' began.

The Commands involved were:

South East Asia Command (SEAC) under the direction of the Supreme Commander, Admiral Lord Louis Mountbatten;

Allied Land Forces South East Asia (ALFSEA);

Air Command South East Asia (ACSEA);

Ceylon Army Command (CAC);

Eastern Air Command (EAC);

The Commander-in-Chief Eastern Fleet;

the Admiralty;

and the Air Ministry.

At an early stage in the planning, the Commander-in-Chief Eastern Fleet offered the use of an aircraft carrier to fly off a Spitfire Squadron as soon as the airstrip became available. No. 132 Squadron was earmarked for this role and preparations were put in hand to train the pilots in the art of deck take-offs, but because of the delay in making a final decision to develop the islands into an air base, the ultimate date for completion of the airstrip intruded into planned naval operations in which the carrier would be needed and the offer was withdrawn. No. 132 Squadron's participation in 'Operation Pharos' was cancelled.

No. 217, a torpedo carrying Beaufighter Squadron, was also given advanced notice of a move to RAF 'Brown', still an unknown location, for operations over the Indian Ocean. The decision to base Beaufighters on the islands was made because the planners, on the basis of intelligence reports, surmised that, once the Japanese became aware that the Cocos Islands were being developed as an air base, their likely reaction would be to mount an air attack using an estimated four flying boats or twelve medium bombers or possibly a bombardment by elements of the Japanese fleet's heavy units carrying up to one battalion of troops to destroy the existing installations on the islands. It was also surmised that once the torpedo-carrying aircraft became operational, the risk of the Japanese making an attack would be reduced.

As the Beaufighters would be required to fly considerable distances, both to get to their new base and when carrying out operations from the islands, tests were commenced with a view to increasing the range and efficiency of the aircraft's engines. To conduct these experiments an Engineer was flown from the Bristol Aircraft Company's factory in the United Kingdom to the Squadron's base at Vavuniya, India.

The tests showed that in still air the range of the aircraft could be increased to 2,100 miles if the aircraft was fitted with drop tanks, but in the Far East at that time these tanks were at a premium. After much deliberation, a decision was made to cancel the move in view of a dramatic decline in Japanese naval activity in the Indian ocean and doubts as to the practicability of using Beaufighters for long distance offensive operations. By the time that the decision was made, some 24 aircrews had completed training for the operation.

While the engine tests were being made and the aircrew were completed their training, a Sergeant and 14 Other Ranks of No. 7217 Service Echelon, No. 217 Squadon's ground staff, became the first RAF men to land on the Cocos Islands as part of 'Operation Pharos'. The small group were firstly sent to SEAC Headquarters at Kandy, Ceylon, where they were given a course in field hygiene followed by instructions in the mixing of Dichloro-Diphenyl-Trichloroethane (DDT) and kerosene to make a very efficient spray for controlling mosquitoes and other flying insects.

On completing the course they were informed that their final destination was still a top secret and given lectures on security with a warning of the dire consequences should they be guilty of breaching that security. Their job would be the spraying of the DDT mixture over large areas of jungle to reduce the hazard to health by insect-borne diseases.

On 24th February 1945, the small group were taken to Colombo where they embarked on HMCS *Uganda*. On leaving the harbour, the ship set sail into the Indian Ocean on a southerly course. The following day they were informed that their destination was the Cocos Islands where they would put into practice their newly taught skills.

John Porter, was a member of this unit and clearly remembers their landing on the islands on 28th February 1945. Laden with small kit, rifles and ammunition, they clambered down rope netting that was draped over the side of the ship into native boats that were bobbing about on the heavy swell many feet below the level of the deck and were ferried ashore to Direction Island where they were greeted by a few Army men and some of the civilians from the cable station, who arranged accommodation and fed them.

The following day the party were met by an Army Medical Officer who supervised the mixing of the DDT and kerosene. They were split into groups and ferried to the various islands. John went to one of the smaller islands, Horsburgh, where there was a small detachment of Indian troops, part of the islands garrison and a few Royal Navy men who were engaged in planting anchorage points and laying down marker buoys.

On completing their task on Horsbugh Island they rejoined the main group on West Island, the largest, where men of the Royal Engineers and Pioneer Companies had commenced to drive a road through the jungle to the commencement of the proposed airstrip and to clear an area ready for a Royal Artillery heavy anti aircraft battery. The RAF men spent most of their time on this island, which was over 7 miles long and less than a mile in width, until they had completed their hot, sticky but essential task.

During their short stay on the islands they existed on typical front line rations of tea, bully beef, jam and biscuits. Sometimes joining the Army men, from whom they scrounged material to construct beds and other comforts, in impromptu games.

By the time that they had completed their task on the islands the posting of No. 217 Squadron had been cancelled and they were returned to the squadron in India.

Seven small cargo ships that had spent their life trading between ports in the Far East were earmarked to take part in 'Operation Pharos' and a provisional time-table was produced. The ships were the SS *Salween*, SS *Rajula*, SS *Islami*, SS *Santami*, SS *Jalagopal*, SS *Maharajah* and the SS *Dilwara*. A number of other vessels were to be used as required including several small tankers to carry the thousands of gallons of oil and aviation spirit that would be needed for the re-fuelling of aircraft once the base became operational.

Those vessels sailing from Indian ports were given the code name 'Sinker' and those from ports in Ceylon, 'Cockroach'. In due course each ship's cargo and the kit of the men sailing in them were marked with the respective code names.

At the end of January 1945, an alarming report was received from Air Command South East Asia, that Germany was reinforcing the Japanese war effort in the South Pacific or South China Seas with 'U' Boats. These submarines could be based in Java or Sumatra and their likely route across the Indian Ocean to get to these bases could well converge with that of the 'Pharos' convoy at a point 200 miles to the west of the Cocos Islands.

An embargo was placed on any ship sailing before 15th February, the main convoy being scheduled to sail from Indian ports on 17th March (D-Day being March 30th 1945).

As the time for the sailing of the convoy drew nearer, Naval Intelligence Officers became aware that with the progress of the war turning in favour of the Allies, many Japanese naval units were being withdrawn from the Indian Ocean. As the overall picture of Japanese activities in the Indian Ocean became clear, previous plans were revised and it was decided that it would be reasonably safe for the seven vessels allocated to the convoy to sail as independent units without an escort.

By permitting the ships to sail independently, a number of Royal Navy escort vessels would be released to take part in the invasion of Akyab Island, off the coast of Burma, an operation which was scheduled to take place at the same time as 'Operation Pharos'.

As the men and units were selected for the coming operation, they were subjected to very strict security precautions. All mail, parcels, photographs etc were heavily censored. Cameras were required to be packed with the heavy kit, the use of them and the keeping of uncensored diaries being forbidden to all ranks. The log books of all vehicles that were to be used in the move were taken and retained in the custody of unit Transport Officers.

The closing of bank accounts, mess accounts, club membership and personal accounts was forbidden. Where this was necessary, the person concerned was required to send the relevant correspondence to a central collecting box at his unit's headquarters, where it would be sent in one batch to a Base Post Office. There it would be held until the security aspect of the move allowed it to be despatched to it's final destination.

While most of the RAF personnel who would be required to staff the new base were being sent from the United Kingdom to assemble in due course at RAF Station Kalyan, a few miles from the city of Bombay, many other units, mostly Army, were gathering with their equipment at ports in India and Ceylon to sail for, what to them, was an as yet unknown destination. The experiences of these first arrivals was very similar and the reminiscences of Douglas Hatcher, a member of No. 652 Artisan Works Company of the Royal Engineers, will sound all too familiar to those who have been subject of a move during wartime service.

At the end of January 1945, No 652 Artisan Works Company, of No. 164 CRE, was at Tinsulia Tank Farm, Assam, where the men were being instructed in the erection of pre-fabricated petrol and oil storage tanks by Engineers of Petroleum Company No. 700 of the United States Army. With little warning the course was cancelled and the unit and their kit were bundled aboard a train for the long haul across India and down to Colombo, Ceylon, where they boarded the SS *Rajula*. The ship had arrived from Bombay four days earlier and was already loaded with other Royal Engineer units, a Pioneer Company, some Indian troops and a Squadron of the Royal Air Force Regiment.

On 29th March 1945 the ship left Colombo harbour and joined a heavily escorted convoy sailing East. After two days at sea the troops awoke to discover that their ship was sailing alone on the deep blue sea with just flying fish and dolphins for company. There was not another ship in sight and they were sailing in a Southerly direction.

Constructing the airstrip, Cocos Islands, 1945.

A meeting of Officers was held, after which each unit was briefed by it's own Officers who informed the men that their destination was to be the Cocos Islands where they would be engaged in the construction of a Royal Air Force base. They were also informed that the Cocos Islands would be the most advanced Allied air base in South East Asia, the nearest Japanese occupied territory being Christmas Island, some 550 miles to the East, while the nearest friendly country, Ceylon, was 1,700 miles to the North. Almost as an afterthought they were told that there was a possibility that the Japanese might already be in occupation of the islands.

The briefings continued with a short history of the islands, their climatic conditions etc. They were also given information as to the current war situation and assured that security had been so strict that the Japanese were unlike to be aware that an operation was underway.

Douglas says that his unit was composed of tradesmen who regarded themselves as civilians in uniform, with not a soldier among them. When the briefings were over they were left to contemplate the possibility that, armed with nothing more than a few obsolete .303 Lee Enfield rifles and a few rounds of ammunition they might have to face trained and experienced Japanese troops. It was too frightening to contemplate!

On the ship was No. 2962 Squadron of the Royal Air Force Regiment which had been specially formed at the Regimental Depot at Secunderabad, India, for 'Operation Pharos' as a light anti-aircraft unit. The squadron was armed with 18 sets of twin Browning .303 machine guns and 16 Hispano 22mm guns. It would form part of the island's air defence system together with the heavy anti-aircraft guns of No. 37/13 Battery of the Royal Indian Artillery.

All the Royal Air Force personnel who were engaged in 'Operation Pharos' were given training in ground defence prior to embarking. They would be armed with rifles, Sten guns, Lewis guns, machine carbines, grenades and would be in support of the 800 men of the 26/14 Punjabi Regiment.

No. 2962 Squadron comprised 7 Officers and 142 Other Ranks under the command of Squadron Leader A.R. Dankes. They had travelled from the Regimental Depot to Kalyan before boarding the SS *Rajula* at Bombay. After a short stop in the harbour at Colombo, the ship set sail, arriving off the Cocos Islands on 3rd April and anchoring some 4 miles out from the lagoon. Group Captain A.W. Hunt, the Fortress Commander, Colonel Harvey the Military Administrator and Wing Commander Bealle, the Staff Officer Administration, went ashore to arrange for the disembarking of the troops.

This was accomplished the following day when landing craft ferried the men, their guns and equipment to the beachhead on the northern tip of West Island. Once ashore the Officers held a conference with Major Cochrane, the islands Anti-Aircraft Defence Officer, to decide on the disposition of the guns.

One flight under Flight Lieutenant J.A. Gee was sent to a point 300 yards south of the landing jetty and six of the 20 mm guns under Flying Officer A.N. Dore were sited at the extreme north of West Island. Two more 20mm guns under Sergeant Dyson were placed on the lagoon side of the proposed site for the heavy anti-aircraft gun battery which was also near to the beachhead. Squadron headquarters was set up near the landing jetty.

Flight Lieutenant Gee then took one Section to Direction Island and a second Section went to Horsburgh Island where they took over some existing positions of an Army Bofors Detachment.

The members of the Squadron worked hard, the sites having to be cleared of dense undergrowth and fallen palm fronds by hand. Despite having to sleep in the open and enduring a heavy fall of rain during the night, the guns were in position and ready for action by dawn on the 6th April. Flight Lieutenant J.M. Bates was made Airfield Defence Officer under the command of Lieutenant Colonel R.C. Robinson, the Ground defence officer and Squadron Leader Bowden was the Station Defence Officer.

Group Captain A.W. Hunt, the Fortress Commander, assumed command of Royal Air Force Station Brown on 3rd April 1945 and three days later was promoted to the rank of Air Commodore. He was well aware of the defence problems posed by the ever present threat of a Japanese attack on the islands, having at one time been the Deputy Director of Ground Defences at the Air Ministry.

Another Army unit which had been withdrawn from Assam was the 86th Indian General Hospital. This unit was to provide a 10 bed hospital for the base and be ready to provide medical care for up to 1,500 casualties should this be necessary following the forthcoming invasion of the islands of the East Indies. Initially they erected their tents near the beachhead but as more equipment and materials became available they moved to the RAF domestic site at the southern end of West Island where, apart from the flying control tower, the unit became the first to acquire permanent buildings.

Although the islands were relatively free from disease, in similar tropical islands in the South Pacific, American troops had been affected with a nasty type of scrub typhus. The use of a chemical named Di-Butyl-Phthalate had been tried out and proved most effective, reducing the incidence of scrub typhus by as much as 75%. This chemical, in liquid form, was issued to all troops while en-route to the Cocos Islands with instructions that it was to be applied by hand on all items of clothing, particularly to the seams of garments. Such was the importance of this instruction that the application of the chemical was supervised by the Officers and Senior NCOs.

When aircraft in transit commenced to land on the islands, instructions were issued that they were to be disinfected prior to leaving their last airfield and again immediately on landing on the Cocos Islands.

As the different units arrived, the men were briefed as to the function of their respective units and of their own particular duties. During the early days of the operation, the daily routine for all branches of the Services was mostly hard manual work, irrespective of trade or rank as priority was given to clearing the sites of scrub and undergrowth for the technical and domestic areas, digging wells and erecting tents and marquees, although the later did not arrive for two weeks. The first priority of the Army units was to clear a road and commence work on the airstrip. The Royal Engineers and Pioneer Corps worked especially hard on this with their bulldozers, graders, levellers etc, knowing that until they had laid sufficient of the airstrip for the Spitfires to become airborne, the increasing number of men arriving on the islands had little to defend themselves with should a Japanese attack develop. With palm trees growing to heights of 70-80 feet and over 110 trees to the acre, this was a big undertaking. For each tree that was destroyed the Ross Estate was paid £1 to partially compensate for the loss of production from the trees which represented the islanders' livelihood. When the base was complete over 18,000 trees had been taken down.

During these early days all new arrivals, officers and men alike, had to sleep in the open, pending the unloading of the tents from the ships and invariably at sometime during most nights there would be a quite heavy tropical rainstorm. Surprisingly, none of the troops appeared to suffer any ill effects from their daily wetting.

There were no wild animals or poisonous reptiles to contend with but very large centipedes could give a nasty bite to the unwary. The large, but harmless land crabs were everywhere and like the rats, became a nuisance, particularly during the night as they climbed over the sleeping men.

The Air Ministry had arranged to supply most of the Royal Air Force personnel to staff the new Station and in December 1944, a large contingent of airmen of all trades embarked on the 45,000 ton liner, *Queen of Bermuda* at Liverpool docks as part of draft No. 9660 destined for No. 129 Staging Post. The ship had been a cruise liner in peacetime, plying between the ports of the West Indies, but her wartime role was as a troopship carrying up to 5,000 troops. On 14th December she sailed as part of a large convoy heading out into the Atlantic Ocean.

Like all wartime overseas postings the move was cloaked in secrecy, the members of the draft only knowing that they had been posted to No. 129 Staging Post. Few were aware of what a Staging Post was. They had been issued with tropical kit but all knew of the perversity of wartime postings, the consensus of opinion being that they were bound for cold climes. On this occasion they were wrong, as a few days later the convoy turned south and then east, to sail through the Straits of Gibraltar and into the Mediterranean Sea.

Christmas Day 1944 was celebrated by the issue of a can of Canadian beer as the ship cruised along the North African coastline with the ship's tannoy commenting on the place names of the distant shore which had been household names during the previous four years. A brief stop was made at Port Said to discharge troops and then the ship moved into the Suez Canal.

The large contingent of homesick troops on board, spent a nostalgic New Year's Eve 1944 anchored in the Bitter Lakes, about halfway along the Canal and on New Year's Day the ship moved on to Suez and into the heat of the Red Sea. A further stop was made at Aden where more troops were discharged and on 12th January 1945, four weeks after leaving wartime Britain, the great ship nosed her way into the harbour at Bombay, the largest city in India, where she tied up opposite the imposing *Gateway of India.*

Draft No. 9660 was transported to the huge RAF transit camp at Worli on the outskirts of Bombay where topees were exchanged for the more sensible bush hats and they were issued with a tropical bed roll consisting of sheets, blankets, a mosquito net and a 'durrah' to wrap them in together with a piece of rope to tie up the bundle. This was carried throughout their service in the Far East.

After two weeks, many of the men were sent to trade schools to brush up on their skills and were also given training in field craft and airfield defence under tropical conditions with emphasis on jungle survival.

Others went to a remote part of the RAF Station at Kalyan, about 50 miles from Bombay and just over the hill from the notorious Deolali, a pre-war Army Station which has been the subject of many Service songs and stories of men going mad with the heat and horrendous tropical diseases.

Gradually getting acclimatised to the heat and conditions in the Far East, the various RAF groups were finally brought together in the camp at Kalyan by 1st March where they remained for a further two weeks. It was from these 600 or so men and at this station that the newest Royal Air Force Station was officially formed. To be known initially by it's code name of Royal Air Force Station 'Brown' it was to be the home of No. 129 Staging Post but security was still very strict and the location of the new station was still not disclosed to the men.

Airfield defence training continued and a mock-up of a combined operations and filter room was made where training was given to S.D. Clerks. A Vengeance aircraft from a nearby training centre was used in conjunction with this training.

On 19th February, work was suspended while search parties were formed to look for a missing airman. He and a companion had gone climbing on a nearby 3,000ft hill and he had fallen and broken both his legs. His companion returned to the camp for help. He was found after several hours, a clue to his location being provided when a number of vultures were seen circling around a particular place.

The composition of the new Station comprised:

The Fortress Commander
Commanding Officer
Administration
Fighter Operations
Intelligence Section
Accounts Section
Chaplain's Department
Armaments Section
Signals Section
Radar Section
Marine Craft Section
Messing
Daily Servicing Squadron & Squadron HQ
Flying Control
Medical Section

Anti Gas Section
Postal Section
Physical Training Section
Motor Transport Section
Provost Section
Service Wing HQ
Mobile Salvage Unit
Repair & Salvage Section
Station Workshops
Repair & Inspection/Squadron HQ
Welfare
Meteorological Section

No 129 Staging Post comprised:

Commanding Officer	*State Room*
Headquarters	*Reinforcing Aircraft*
	Daily Servicing Squadron/HQ
Briefing Section	*Reinforcing Aircraft*
	Servicing Squadron HQ

The composition was the same as the majority of RAF flying Stations with the addition of the Marine Section.

The fundamental control of the Station was with HQ ACSEA and the administrative control was with the AOC No. 222 Group. All the equipment was supplied by DHQ Ceylon.

Security was tightened up in India and Ceylon, special security squads being formed to listen to Service talk in clubs, hotels and cafes. As 'D' Day approached, servicemen were continually warned against talking about service matters to civilians.

On 18th March 1945, the main RAF party was taken from the camp at Kalyan to the docks at Bombay where they boarded the three ships, SS *Rajula*, SS *Jalagopal* and SS *Salween* for the final stages of their journey to the unknown location of No. 129 Staging Post. All three ships sailed independently to Ceylon where they anchored in the harbour at Colombo.

The history of the SS *Salween* was similar to the other two ships. Built in 1937, she was of 9,360 tons and owned by Henderson Brothers of Glasgow. She had been engaged in carrying general cargo between Glasgow, Rangoon and other ports throughout the Far East. When war broke out she was hastily converted to carry troops and the RAF contingent were only a few of the many thousands that she had previously carried as was testified by the hundreds of names and initials that were carved on every inch of the ship's handrails and woodwork.

After several days, the troops were taken ashore and marched through the city in one long column along the Galle Face Promenade. They came to a stretch of sandy beach where they were able to cavort in the warm tropical seas and wash away the sweat and grime that had accumulated since leaving Kalayan.

Five days after arriving at Colombo the three ships sailed at intervals and unescorted to their final destination, the Cocos Islands. The troops were not informed of this until the ships had been at sea for two days and then the briefings began. Although the Allies had gone onto the offensive in Burma and throughout the Pacific islands, the Japanese war machine was as active as ever and the information that they were destined for an isolated group of islands, far from any other Allied base, with no air cover and very little armament for defence other than what they carried with them, brought home to them that the three months of leisurely perambulations to the Far East was at an end and they could find themselves in action as ground troops in a very short space of time.

On the evening of 5th April the SS *Salween*, which carried most of the Signals and Radar personnel, reached the Cocos Islands but too late to commence unloading that day. She cruised slowly around during the night ready for an early disembarkation the following morning. Everyone was up by first light to catch a glimpse of their new home. So low were the islands that, as the ship drew nearer they appeared as just a line of palm trees growing out of the sea.

The ship anchored some 4 miles from the beachhead and scrambling nets were hung over the sides. A fleet of landing craft sailed out to meet the ship and the disembarkation began. It was no easy matter to clamber down the steep sides of the ship into a craft which was rising and falling on the heavy swell while laden with small kit and encumbered with a rifle and 160 rounds of ammunition, however it was accomplished without mishap and the move to West Island began.

On reaching the beachhead the men were divided into parties of eight and a tin of Compo rations, sufficient for 24 hours, was distributed among each group. The RAF domestic site was at the opposite end of the island, seven miles from the beachhead and as each group received their rations they were pointed in a southerly direction and told to start walking with their small kit and weapons. Their kitbags containing the rest of their uniforms and equipment would follow later.

Although only 12° south of the Equator, the walk, it could hardly be called a march, was not too arduous for the fit young men who had full water bottles and an unlimited supply of coconut juice.

The word 'juice' is used intentionally as the nuts may be used at various stages of growth and at each stage their contents differ. In the very young green nuts the liquid inside the husks, before the nutshell is formed, is very bitter, somewhat similar to white vinegar. As the nut develops, this liquid becomes effervescent, rather like lemonade and is most refreshing. The next stage is the fully ripe nut with the inner shell containing the milk formed inside the husk as we in the West know it. Finally, when the ripe nut has fallen from the tree, it is likely to start sprouting, at which time the milk solidifies, becoming much like marshmallow which the islanders call 'Tombong'. It is a tasty and very nourishing food which is given to babies and young children.

On arriving at the domestic site, the men were put to work clearing the undergrowth by hand in order to settle down for the night and to prepare the ground for the arrival of the tents, but they did not appear for nearly two weeks. Sleep that night was in the open under the stars and the inevitable heavy rainstorm.

The following day groups were formed to clear sites in the domestic and technical areas. Others were detailed for guard duties and fire pickets, fire being a very real hazard. When the tents finally arrived four men were allocated to each. Water was rationed to 1 gallon per man per day but as more wells became available this was increased to 2 gallons and a water tender visited the various sites several times a day.

The work was supervised by Warrant Officer Bellerby, the Station Warrant Officer (SWO). A peacetime Regular, he was typical of the best of his breed. As strict as conditions permitted, he was very fair and knew how to get the best out of men who were not used to hard manual labour and were of a Service that was not renowned for being tolerant of disciplinarians.

An incident which occurred shortly after the arrival of the tents, illustrates the man's sense of humour. He was working in his office (tent) when two corporals marched in one of the 470 Indian Enrolled Followers who had been allocated to the RAF.

"I will not work. Even if you beat me, I will not work!" protested the Indian.

The Warrant Officer made no comment and carried on writing.

The Indian continued to shout "You can shoot me, but I will still not work!"

Without raising his head the Warrant Officer quietly said to the Corporals, "Alright then, take him out and shoot him."

The Indian immediately fell to his knees and said, "Sorry Sahib, don't shoot me, I will work!"

Warrant Officer Bellerby just smiled and continued with his writing…

Regulation dress was khaki shorts, bush jackets with the sleeves rolled up, bush hats, khaki stockings and black boots or shoes. After dusk sleeves were rolled down and long slacks were worn. In practice, during working hours jackets or shirts were discarded and only the briefest of clothes were worn. On the domestic sites even shorts were often left off in favour of a towel wrapped around the waist. Initially the Army was not so fortunate as the RAF as their scale of kit did not include shorts. The Fortress Commander arranged for this to be altered, bringing all troops on to the same kit scale. Surrounded by sea, there was plenty of scope for swimming but it was essential to wear some sort of footwear when in the water as coral cuts took a very long time to heal. The tour of duty for RAF men was fixed at 6 months with the option of extending it to 12 months.

The 'Sinker' and 'Cockroach' ships had begun to arrive from 22nd March and the base developed at a rapid rate although bad weather hampered the unloading of some of the early arrivals. By 3rd April, 3,300 men were ashore, 80% of the heavy equipment and 820 tons of stores had been discharged while 200 yards of the airstrip had been cleared of trees and undergrowth.

Five days later, all 6,263 personnel were ashore together with 2,250 tons of stores, and 800 yards of airstrip had been cleared and levelled, ready for the laying of the pierced steel plating (PSP), which was to form the top surface.

While the development of West Island was forging ahead, on Direction Island the Marine Section was also getting established. They were equipped with three High Speed Launches (HSL's), No. 2707, No. 2562, and No. 2698, for air/sea rescue duties, the latter two boats were new and had been shipped out from the United Kingdom. There was also one 60ft General Service Pinnace, four 24ft Marine Tenders and a number of bomb scows. All the marine craft had been transported to the islands by the SS *Bel Pareil*.

On an island base a Marine Section was invaluable. Apart from manning the high speed rescue launches, they crewed the tenders which were used for servicing the flying boats, ran a daily boat service carrying mail and personnel between the units on the various islands. The unit also supplied a crew for the 'Wrangles', an additional boat which was hired from the Ross Estates to supplement the RAF boats.

Crews were allocated and a duty roster introduced. The high speed launches were on call at all times and later, when the

Liberator bombers were airborne on operations, they patrolled the known route of the bombers to provide a sea rescue service if required. The three launches rotated over a three day period, each launch doing 24 hours as duty launch, 24 hours on standby duty and then 24 hours on maintenance. Each of these 65ft high-speed launches were fitted with three 500-horsepower Napier engines and were capable of speeds of 28-30 knots in calm water but with the huge swells that were to be found in the waters of the Indian Ocean, often reaching 20ft between peaks, they were seldom able to exceed double figures with safety.

Each launch was normally crewed by a 1st and 2nd Coxswain, 3 Deckhands, 2 Marine Fitters, 1 Wireless Operator/Mechanic, 1 Wireless Operator to operate the 1154/55 Marconi transmitter/receiver, the same type of radio apparatus as was fitted on many British aircraft and a Hospital Orderly trained in first aid.

For their size the launches carried quite a formidable sting in the form of twin turrets on top of the superstructure and a 20mm Oerlikon cannon with an armoured shield on the stern. When required, two ½ inch Browning machine guns, one each side of the boat, could be quickly erected.

The fuel tanks of the boats were kept topped up at all times with 1,800 gallons of fuel. This had to be loaded manually using a hand operated swivel pump from 47 gallon drums. The Catalina flying boats carried a similar amount of fuel and the Marine Section had to help manhandle it into the tanks high in the wings, unfortunately this fuel was supplied in 4 gallon cans, which made it a long and difficult operation.

Initially the boat crews lived aboard their craft but as tents and then permanent buildings became available only the crew of the duty launch stayed on board during their tour of duty. Apart from the difficulty of re-fuelling, the members of the Marine Section had other problems to deal with. There was no slipway facilities, no moorings for the launches, water was short and they had to feed themselves on dry rations. The members of the unit were not without resources and pressed into service members of a nearby Royal Engineers unit to repair some old Victorian rolling stock on rusty rails and to put into working order an equally rusty and dilapidated crane on a crumbling jetty for their use.

The RAF Marine Section originally came into being at the end of World War 1 under the control of the Admiralty when motor-boat crews were used to supply and service the new breed of flying-boats but it was not until 1940 that air sea rescue was conceived and developed by Coastal Command using High Speed Launches in conjunction with patrolling aircraft to initiate a fully comprehensive organisation of Air Sea Rescue.

The Royal Air Force air sea rescue units throughout the world were allocated a recognition number similar to a squadron number yet no such number was given to the Marine Section on the Cocos Islands. Perhaps this was another ploy to help maintain the secrecy of the island base.

On the 6th April 1945 Group Captain Hunt received promotion to Air Commodore, he also received a new directive from Air Command South East Asia setting out his responsibilities as Fortress Commander and naming the units that he would have under his control. The directive read:

(1). You will be responsible for the development of an airfield and air facilities capable of fulfilling the following functions;

(a) An air staging post.

(b) Offensive and special operations.

(c) General reconnaissance.

(d) Air Defence.

(e) Air sea rescue.

(f) Detailed instructions will follow regarding the development of the airfield and air operations to be conducted from RAF Brown.

(2) LOCAL DEFENCE.
You are appointed Fortress Commander.

(3) COMMAND AND DISCIPLINE.
You will exercise powers of command and discipline (but not punishment in the case of Naval and Military personnel), over all British Forces on Brown.

(4) ADMINISTRATION.
Ceylon Army Command have been made responsible for the maintenance of all forces on Brown,(including Naval Forces),to the extent for which the Army is normally responsible for the maintenance of Army and RAF Forces in the field. All other maintenance for RAF and the provision of purely RAF equipment will be the responsibility of No. 222 Group, Indian Ocean, who will arrange shipment in conjunction with Ceylon Army Command. All Naval maintenance and Naval supplies will be the responsibility of the Commander-in-Chief, Eastern Fleet.

(5) CIVIL AFFAIRS.
To assist, you will have attached to your staff a Civil Affairs Officer.

(6) ROYAL NAVAL ATTACHMENT.

(7) ARMY.
103 Field Cash Office.

ARTILLERY.
37/13 Ind. Heavy AA Battery.

ENGINEERS.
HQ 164 CRE Works.
91 E & M Platoon.
652 Artisan Works Company.
685 Artisan Works Company.
70 M.E. Platoon.
51 Bomb Disposal Platoon. Indian Engineers.

INFANTRY
26/14 Punjab.

SUPPLY AND TRANSPORT.
638 Indian Supply Section.
352 Petrol Depot Platoon. Lt. RASC i/c.
73 Indian Field Bakery Section.
115 Indian Field Butchery Section.
536 Indian Fire Fighting Section.

MEDICAL.
86 Indian General Hospital.
24 Indian Field Hygiene Section.
42 Indian Dental Unit (BT).

(8) ORDNANCE.
Det. 204 Indian B.O.D.
Det. 16. Mobile Laundry and Bath Unit.
ELECTRICAL & MECHANICAL ENGINEERS.
Det. Indian Electrical & Mechanical Engineers.

TRANSPORTATION.
243 Indian Dock Operating Company.
220 Indian Port Construction Company.
270 Indian Port Operating Company.

LABOUR.
1282 Indian Pioneer Company.
1465 Indian Pioneer Company.
1545 Indian Pioneer Company.

POSTAL.
46 Indian Field Post Office.

MISCELLANEOUS.
2nd Indian Base Sanitation Section.

Det. Static Cinema.

Det. E.F.I.Ceylon.

(9) ROYAL AIR FORCE.

RAF Station Cocos Islands.

No. 129 Staging Post.

No. 136 Fighter Squadron.

No. 7136 Service Echelon.

No. 217 Beaufighter Squadron. (Later cancelled)

No. 7217 Service Echelon. (Later cancelled)

No. 15 M.S.U.(T).

No. 2962 AA Squadron RAF Regiment.

No. 78 Embarkation Unit.

No. 737 Forecasting Centre.

No. 216 Indian Wing Signals Section.

No. 240 Indian Line Section.

410 Indian Enrolled Followers are allocated to the RAF.

Living conditions continued to be primitive for all ranks as tents did not become available until the 15th of the month but the work of clearing the undergrowth on the domestic and technical sites progressed rapidly as did the clearing and laying of the airstrip, which had first priority.

A danger beneath the trees was that of falling coconuts which, weighing over 10lbs and falling from a height of 70 feet, could cause serious injuries. The tinned rations provided were on the Ceylon scale of rationing and soon proved to be inadequate for men engaged in heavy manual work in the tropics. This was soon changed to the more liberal Indian ration scale which was more in keeping with the requirements of the Cocos Islands personnel.

The land crabs, which were quite harmless, were so numerous that there was wholesale slaughter of them, particularly on the domestic sites, until an order was issued forbidding this as their dead carcases attracted flies despite the liberal use of DDT and also because the islands water supply was only just below the surface.

Landing craft used to bring men and materials ashore during the construction of the airbase in 1945.

On 9th April, the mobile radar units detected an unidentified aircraft flying at an estimated height of 20,000 feet. It turned away to the south before getting too close to the islands. As a result of this scare, a Chance Light was installed at the commencement of the airstrip so that work could carry on unchecked throughout the night.

The same day the ex-United Kingdom men received their first delivery of mail which arrived via the flying boats of 240 and 191 Squadrons. The mail continued to arrive twice weekly on Mondays and Thursdays throughout the life of the RAF Station.

As the unloading of the ships proceeded, many matters of a frustrating nature were revealed. Stores had been loaded in a 'non-tactical' manner (i.e. those marked XX, the highest priority, had been loaded first, consequently they were the last to be unloaded). This applied to all the ships. As a result, the first items to reach No. 129 Staging Post's HQ from the beachhead were a piano and some library books. The nine Officers and 320 Other Ranks of the 37/13 HAA Battery had worked long and hard to get their guns in position, but were left without ammunition as this arrived on a later ship. Few hand tools arrived and large amounts of stores had been pilfered at the docks prior to being loaded.

Any major Service operation entails an enormous amount of planning, but it does seem that very often when that planning is put into practice some military men do not learn from the mistakes of their predecessors. In the Suez campaign of 1956 and again 37 years later on the Falkland Islands troops suffered unnecessarily through non tactical loading of equipment.

By 22nd April, two piers of 300 feet and 150 feet had been completed at the beachhead, which greatly assisted the landing of stores from the landing craft, in particular the crated Spitfires of No. 136 Squadron. These were ferried ashore and then transported the six miles to the airstrip, where the men of No. 7136 Service Echelon, the Squadron's ground staff, worked feverishly to get the machines ready for air testing.

By 24th April, eight machines had been re-assembled and by 26th April a further 800 yards of pierced steel plating had been laid. At 0945 hours that day, Squadron Leader Soga, No. 136 Squadron's Commanding Officer, took off in the first of the Spitfires to be air tested, within a few hours all sixteen aircraft plus four spares had been air tested.

As the Spitfires became airborne and the sound of their Rolls Royce Merlin engines echoed over the islands, cheers could be heard arising from all parts of the base as the apprehension of the previous weeks faded with the knowledge that should the Japanese mount an attack on the islands they would now be faced with the formidable mobile gun platforms of the Spitfires as opposed to the single static heavy anti-aircraft battery and the light guns of the RAF Regiment.

The Mark VIII Spitfires were fitted with a Merlin 61 engine developing 1520 horsepower, giving a ceiling of 44,000 ft, a range of 1,180 miles and a speed of 408 mph at 25,000ft, superior to any aircraft the Japanese had at that time. The Squadron had an impressive tally of enemy aircraft destroyed before it arrived on the Cocos Islands, but as the pilots had not been flying for several weeks they were immediately put on an intensive flying programme to get them up to top form.

With the Spitfires becoming operational, a combined filter room Operating Procedure order was issued containing instructions as to the required state of readiness expected from the squadron. This was to be effective from 15 minutes after first light until 30 minutes before last light. The standby aircraft were expected to be airborne within 1 minute of an alarm and two sections to be at readiness and be airborne within 3 minutes. Other aircraft were to be at 15, 30 and 60 minutes notice.

The men of No. 7136 Echelon soon utilised the huge packing cases in which the aircraft fuselages had been shipped. Under their Commanding Officer, Flight Lieutenant A.C.C. Fairman, the cases were turned into workshops for the various trade sections, Electrical, Accounts, Wireless, Armaments, Photographic, Equipment, etc. A tyre bay was constructed and two marquees were erected for the CO and the unit's Orderly Room staff.

CHAPTER 9

RAF Station 'Brown' and No. 129 Staging Post

ALTHOUGH RAF STATION 'BROWN' was officially formed at RAF Station Kalyan, India on 3rd January 1945, as the previous pages show, it remained in the embryo stage for several weeks; gathering and training the personnel and units who arrived as part of No. 129 Staging Post until the main group sailed on divers dates towards the end of March, re-uniting on the Cocos Islands during the first week of April with Wing Commander D.T. Macpherson as Station Commander.

In the beginning, the personnel of the various RAF units worked together to clear the ground, but as equipment began to arrive from the beachhead they concentrated on setting up their own Sections on the sites allocated to them and by 14th April everyone was under canvas and numerous marquees had been erected to accommodate the Station Headquarters, signals centre, workshops etc.

On 19th April, the Flying Control staff had pitched tents and opened a 24-hour listening watch on VHF radio and No.129 Staging Post had opened an air booking centre to allocate seats on the Catalina flying boats of 205, 240 and 191 Squadrons, which maintained the link between the Cocos Islands, Ceylon and Australia.

The Operations Room equipment arrived and they opened a 24 hour watch on 26th April, the same day No.30 RAF Postal

Section became established and 20 RAF Mess's were in operation throughout the islands.

Pilot Officer Hurry, the Officer i/c the RAF Motor Transport Section and his men were kept extremely busy as all the Army lorries were u/s and had to be towed ashore, leaving the RAF transport to do the majority of transporting equipment from the beachhead. A personnel carrier and the RAF fire tenders were also u/s and had to be completely overhauled before they could be used.

On 24th April the first pay parade was held but it was not until 1st May when the P.S.I. opened its first canteen on the domestic site, that this money could be spent. The canteen gave a limited service, selling mostly canned fruit, biscuits, razorblades, soap, etc. A ration of cigarettes and tobacco was supplied free and the first of a weekly beer ration was also supplied.

The 1st May 1945 also saw the publication of Royal Air Force Station Brown's first set of Standing Orders. These were soon followed by regular Daily Routine Orders (DROs).

During the initial stages of 'Operation Pharos', strict radio silence was observed, even by the regular flying boats of No's 205, 240 and 191 Squadrons who daily made the long flight from Ceylon, arriving shortly after dawn to land on the lagoon with their essential supplies, mail and personnel. As the ground clearance progressed, aerials were erected and transmitters and receivers installed. As soon as the fighters of No. 136 Squadron became operational a VHF channel was opened and these instructions were slightly relaxed.

Station Headquarters was established approximately halfway down the eastern side of the strip and the signal section was attached to it. Point to Point W/T was established with Ceylon and Australia and within a short time, watches were opened on three wavelengths covering the 24 hours.

The Flying Control tower was built on the opposite side of the airstrip and was the first of the permanent buildings to be erected. It was built of coral and cement and the front was adorned with the words, 'Cocos 3 feet' in large letters, indicating the height of the airstrip above mean sea level.

For most of the time the work was hard and pressure was maintained to get the Station up to operational readiness. It had its lighter moments, as shown by the Station's daily log, which records that a report was received from the Radar Officer on Horsburgh Island that a goat had eaten his copy of Standing Orders.

The Mobile Radar Units of the AMES's gradually became operational but it was not until the middle of June that the Radar Chain was completed with GCI(COB) and type's 57 and 61 being the main sets. As early as 24th April a medium frequency beacon operating on 375 Kcs with the call sign 'Fox Sugar' had been established and was to prove a boon to incoming aircraft.

With the announcement that the war in Europe was over, an extra ration of beer was issued and 10th May was given over to a day of celebrations. All those who could be spared from duty were given a day off. A Church Service for all Denominations was held beside the airstrip in the morning and sports and games were held during the afternoon. A terse announcement in Routine Orders from the Fortress Commander indicated that, although the war in the West was over he expected that there would be no relaxing of effort against the Japanese and that we had to prepare for what was to come. The next three months were to show that aircraft from the Cocos Island base were well and able to take the war to the enemy.

On 12th May the final draft for 129 Staging Post arrived on the SS *Maharaja*. When the ship sailed four days later, it took with it the detachment of No. 7217 Service Echelon, who had done such sterling work with their DDT spray during the early days of the operation, to rejoin their parent Squadron in India, whose posting to the islands had been cancelled.

On 20th May, one of No. 136 Squadron's Spitfires, 'T', made a heavy landing and overturned. Fortunately the pilot's injuries were slight and the members of No. 7136 Echelon were quick to utilise the aircraft for spares.

Plans for a second runway were cancelled and instead of two 2,000 yard strips it had been decided to have one of 3,500 yards. By 22nd May the first phase of the airstrip had been completed and this day saw the arrival of the first heavy aircraft to land on the newly completed airstrip. The aircraft was a Canso (the amphibious version of the Catalina flying boat) of No. 321 (Dutch) Squadron, piloted by Lieutenant Commander Aerant of the Royal Netherlands Naval Air Service. With a five man crew and six passengers they had flown from the squadron's base at China Bay, Ceylon in a flight time of 15 hours 35 minutes. Also on the 14th, another Canso, 'S' of No. 191 Squadron, flown by Flight Lieutenant Kenny arrived bringing with him Air Vice Marshal Cole who was making a tour of inspection.

Sadly, on 30th May, Aircraftman Charles Ward and Leading Aircraftman Valence Edward Douglas Weir, both of No 129 Staging Post, were reported missing. They were believed to have ventured on to the reef off West Island and been swept away by the ceaselessly pounding 20 foot high waves. No trace of either man was ever found.

The first Liberator aircraft landed on 31st May. These were KH 185 and KH 195, both of No 232 Squadron and were en route from Ceylon to Australia. While the crews and passengers were fed the men of No. 129 Staging Post serviced and refuelled the aircraft ready for a night take off by the light of goose-necked flares. They made the return flight on the 6th June.

As more multi-engined aircraft passed through the islands, breaking the long flight between Ceylon and Australia, No. 129 Staging Post commenced to function, supplying food and accommodation to the weary passengers and crews, servicing the aircraft and giving briefings for the onward flight.

An important part of the briefings was the passing on of weather information.

To supply this information, No. 737 Forcast Centre was established and given the directive that their function was;

(1) To intercept wireless broadcasts of weather from Ceylon, Australia and India.

(2) To transmit its own weather data to both terminals, airports and aircraft in flight.

(3) To arrange interchanges of route and landing forecasts with each terminal to enable the best possible briefing to be given to the aircrew before take off.

(4) As the distance between terminals vary between 1500 and 2000 miles and there is no weather reporting stations in between, it is essential to commence long range flights, working from both ends and also from the Cocos Islands.

In anticipation of an increasing number of flying boat landings on the lagoon, an instruction was received from HQ ACSEA to increase the number of flying boat moorings to a six buoy capacity allowing for three air/sea rescue Catalinas, aircraft in transit and flying boat transport services.

Estimates were also made for the supply of 100 octane petrol for operational aircraft and aircraft in transit to be increased from 323,000 gallons in June to 988,000 gallons in August and then to maintain the monthly supply at 1,000,000 gallons.

As aircraft movements increased an extensive range of radio navigational aids became essential. This had been foreseen and by the time that the base became fully operational it had established the following;

(a) MF Beacon.

(b) HF/DF Station.

(c) VHF/DF Station.

(d) ASV Radar Beacon.

(e) Eureka Beacon.

(f) HF/RT Airfield Control.

(g) VHF/DF Airfield Control.

A Loran beam directed to Malaya and to Ceylon was later installed to act as a long distance homing device. Visual beacons and two floodlights were also available to assist night landings. When the Radar Chain was complete there were five AMES units in position.

For security purposes, all aircraft approaching the islands were instructed to adhere strictly to fundamental procedures, showing their IFF (identification friend or foe) and to fly at a mandatory height of 3,000 feet from 80 miles distance. These instructions remained in force until the end of the war with Japan.

The operators of the Radar units were very efficient in plotting aircraft at extreme range. On the 4th June, MRU 366 plotted one Liberator at 62 miles distance and two Mosquitos at 75 miles. The type 6 L/W AMES 6214 were averaging plots of 55-60 miles, the type 15 GCI AMES 8545 averaged 40-50 miles and the type 57 AMES 14033 plotted frequently over a distance of 200 miles at a range of 132 miles.

On the 5th June, the aircraft carrier HMS *Implacable* en-route to Australia, was plotted from 29 miles to 44 miles. The carrier flew off five Seafires of No. 800 Squadron, Fleet Air Arm and using F24 vertical cameras they made a complete photographic record of the islands. When these were developed, an Avenger aircraft dropped copies for the information of the Fortress Commander.

Before the radio navigational aids were fully available, Lord Louis Mountbatten, the Supreme Commander, South East Asia Command, (SEAC) requested that a detachment of photographic reconnaissance Mosquitos of the Royal Australian Air Force be sent to the islands to obtain up to date photographic information of the Japanese positions in the Netherlands East Indies and Malaya.

No. 87 Squadron RAAF was selected to provide a detachment of three aircraft and crews for this operation which was classified as top secret. The three crews chosen were Squadron Leader K.J. Gray DFC and his navigator Bill Sidlow, MD in a Mk XVI Mosquito. Flight Lieutenant Ron Langford DFC and Flying Officer G. Tozer also in a Mk XVI and Flight Lieutenant A.L.M. Spurgin DFC with Flying Officer L.C. Cobb as his navigator in a Mk 40.

The crews were ordered to fly from their base at Coomale Creek, some 50 miles south of Darwin in the Northern Territories to an airfield near Learmouth on Exmouth Gulf in Western Australia, a flight time of 5 hours, where they would be told their final destination.

Arriving at Leamouth they stayed overnight and the following day were told that their mission was to operate a photographic reconnaissance unit from the Cocos Islands. Given their final briefing they were issued with copies of United States Air Force maps of the Pacific Ocean which included that part of the Indian Ocean showing the position of the Cocos Islands. Their flight plan estimated flight of 5h hours duration by dead reckoning and the weather was predicted as fair. Strict radio silence was to be observed as no W/T was operating on the islands but VHF Homing was available.

On 12th June 1945, the three aircraft, fully laden with petrol for the 1,500 mile flight over the sea, took off into a clear blue Australian sky and quickly climbed to 30,000 feet for the first part of their flight. After passing the point of no return, the weather deteriorated with cloud stretching from 20,000 feet down to sea level. Flying above the upper cloud level they could see no sign of a break in any direction. As fuel gauges dropped towards the danger mark, radio silence was broken on the VHF channel and contact was established with the operator on the Cocos Islands. Within a very short time radio reception had deteriorated until only one of the aircraft was able to hear the transmissions. Unsuccessful efforts were made to home on the voice transmissions.

On the RAF Station a flight of Spitfires was scrambled and a quantity of HF/DF equipment which had recently arrived from the beachhead and was still in the process of being erected, was hastily brought into operation.

With the fuel situation getting to a critical stage after nearly 8 hours flying, Flight Lieutenant Langford indicated that he was going to break formation and go below cloud. As he commenced the long descent from 23,000 feet, Flt/Lt C.A. MacDonald, a pilot of No. 136 squadron, located the two remaining Mosquitos and at the same time the D/F Station came on the air and gave a rough bearing, by which time the Spitfire was able to lead them for some 80 miles to the islands, where both made successful landings with their fuel tanks showing empty after a flight time of 8 hours 20 minutes.

In the meantime Flight Lieutenant Langford and Flying Officer Tozer had descended through the cloud and were almost at sea level before they broke into clear air and directly ahead saw the breakers of a reef surrounding an island. This was North Keeling Island, 15 miles from the main group of the Cocos Islands, but with fuel gauges showing empty they had no time to speculate as to their exact location, their only option being to attempt a landing in the shallows between the reef and the shore.

With flaps down, engine throttled back and the nose raised to reduce forward speed as much as possible the Mosquito was gently and successfully landed in the surf. Neither the pilot or navigator were injured and were able to wade ashore where they spent an uncomfortable night before being rescued the following day by a high speed launch.

An enquiry was held into the loss of the Mosquito (No. A52-606) and how the three aircraft became lost and so far off course. It was established that the United States Air Force charts which had been supplied to the navigators were at fault. The location of the Cocos Islands on these charts showed them as being 65 miles from their true position, even so, had the weather been clear, the aircrews would have sighted the islands from the height at which they were flying.

Several days later urgent signals were received from the Air Ministry instructing that every effort was to be made to recover valuable cameras and secret equipment from the crashed aircraft.

On 15th June, Flying Officer Wilkes, the Officer in Charge of the Mobile Salvage Unit, the Station Medical Officer Flight Lieutenant Pike, the Chief Technical Officer and a salvage crew were put ashore on North Keeling Island by one of the Air/Sea Rescue launches.

After a most difficult landing they split into three groups to find the easiest route to reached the crashed Mosquito as whatever was salvaged would have to be manhandled over three miles of rough ground covered with thick undergrowth.

They were able to remove some equipment and transfer it to the launch that day but Flight Sergeant Hopwood, Corporals Wyling, Brown, Keen and LAC's McCann, O'Kane and Jones remained for a further three days to complete the salvage. They had a rough time as when they went to replenish their water bottles they found that the well marked on their chart was dry and they had to rely on coconut milk to quench their thirst. Later one airman was heard to comment that when he went ashore he had never climbed a tree, now he was better than any monkey!

Leading Aircraftman Johnnie Johnson, a wireless operator/mechanic with the Marine Section, was one of those put ashore as part of the salvage team. He was lucky enough to return to base the same day but his record of that first day makes interesting reading.

North Keeling Island lies 15 miles to the north of the main group of islands and is approximately 3 miles long and 1 mile wide, being roughly in a semi circle around a shallow lagoon which is open to the east. It has a fairly steep shoreline and there is no easy landing place. A way had to be found to put the salvage party ashore and the launch spent some time before eventually locating a place on the eastern side which appeared to offer a reasonable chance of reaching the shore although it was some distance from the site of the crashed aircraft which was on the northern side.

A Carley float was used to get the party ashore. This is a raft with a rigid body and strong netting over an open bottom. The raft was secured to the HSL as a safety measure and the some of the party climbed aboard but they had to make several attempts before they were able to overcome the heavy surf and stumble ashore soaking wet. When all were ashore the three groups forced their way through the heavy undergrowth towards the centre of the island where they came to a shallow lagoon which appeared to be a breeding ground for sharks. There were hundreds of these creatures from monsters to baby size. The jungle was so dense that in order to progress forward, the men had to walk through the shallow water around the edge of the lagoon with the smaller sharks making themselves a nuisance by nipping at their ankles, although doing no harm.

On reaching the far side of the lagoon they forced their way through more jungle until they came to a number of shallow pools between the shore and the reef in which a number of huge sharks were basking in the warm water. The Sergeant i/c gave a loud whoop and jumped into the water brandishing a huge knife but the water was too shallow for the sharks to turn on their side to attack and they sped off, apparently more afraid of him than he was of them.

On reaching the remains of the Mosquito, which looked a sorry sight and out of it's element in the salt water, they quickly removed the IFF and some of the more easily accessible equipment before commencing the hot and tiring journey back to the sanctuary of the waiting launch with their spoils.

On reaching the eastern shore, they retrieved the Carley float and attempted to get back through the reef to the waiting launch by pulling on the rope linking the two. It was found impossible to keep the raft on a straight enough course to negotiate the small gap through he reef. In the end they tied another rope to a tree on the shore and by keeping this taut were able to exercise some control over the sideways drift. In this manner and with a great deal of effort they were able to surmount the breakers without capsizing and climb utterly exhausted onto the launch leaving their seven colleagues behind to complete the removal of the remaining equipment.

The bad weather persisted over the islands and the Australian detachment only flew one operation, a photographic reconnaissance flight to Christmas Island, some 550 miles to the East, before returning to Australia.

On the 5th June 1945, the official address of the base was altered from RAF Station Brown to RAF Station Cocos Islands, Ceylon Air Forces. The code name RAF Brown had been in use for several months as a service postal address but such was the degree of secrecy surrounding 'Operation Pharos' and so good was the security covering the Station's location, that for some time a great deal of mail was passed around RAF Postal Units in the Far East marked 'Address not known'.

On the same date the Fortress Commander received new orders showing that from that date the operational and administrative control of some of the units on the islands would transfer from Air Command South East Asia to HQ No. 222 Group, Indian Ocean, who would be responsible for the provisioning of the administration services to those units which were; No. 136 Squadron, No. 7136 Service Echelon, No. 129 Staging Post, No. 78 Embarkation Unit, No. 2962 Squadron RAF Regiment, No. 737 Forecast Centre and the AMES units.

Following the return of No. 87 Squadron to Australia, a detachment of seven Mk. 34 Mosquitos from No. 684 Squadron, RAF Alipore, India, were posted to the islands to carry out photographic reconnaissance missions.

In a change of policy it was decided to base heavy bombers on the islands to carry out strikes against enemy shipping in the East Indies, supply dropping in Malaya and bombing raids as opportunity arose.

No. 99 and No. 356 Squadrons, both equipped with Liberator bombers, were two of the squadrons selected for these operations and were withdrawn from the Burma Front in preparation for the move.

In reference to the supply dropping operations, a signal was received by the Fortress Commander from Brigadier General J.P. McConnell (USAAF) the Senior Air Staff Officer, HQ ACSEA confirming that S.D. operations were to be mounted from the Cocos Islands and would cover the areas of North and South Jahore and Negri Semilan in Malaya, supplying Force 136 (commanded by Colin MacKenzie) and other clandestine organisations operating behind the Japanese lines. It was realised that aircraft operating from the Cocos islands would be able to carry a far greater load than those at present operating from Ceylon, due to the shorter distances involved. The S.D. operations were to be undertaken by No. 99 Squadron and were to take priority over all other targets.

It was also announced that when these operations commenced, the Headquarters of No. 231 Group would move to the Cocos Islands where they would replace the Fortress Headquarters and No. 175 Wing, Commanded by Group Captain J.C. Sissons DFC, would take over the duties of the Station Headquarters. Fortress Headquarters and Station Headquarters Cocos Islands, would then be disbanded and the Command would transfer to the A.O.C. No. 231 Group who would be responsible to HQ Air Command South East Asia for all forces on the Cocos Islands.

On lst June 1945, it was reported in Station Routine Orders that Wing Commander H.O.M. Bealle, the Officer Commanding No. 129 Staging Post, had been awarded the D.S.O. Later in the month he received a Mention in Dispatches in the King's Birthday Honours.

On 23rd June, two of No. 136 Squadron's Spitfires collided in mid air while on an excercise. Flight Lieutenant Jefferson, flying in aircraft No. MT.989, had the propeller of his aircraft break off, but he made a successful landing on the airstrip. Flying Officer Chowns was not so lucky, his aircraft No. MT 704 became unflyable and he had to take to his parachute, landing in the sea about 5 miles from the islands. The collision had been seen by members of No. 2962 Squadron, RAF Regiment, one of their duties being to keep watch on aircraft in flight. The Air/Sea Rescue unit was notified and HSL 2702 was quickly on the scene. With numerous species of Shark, Barracuda and Giant Rays in the seas around the islands the pilot was fortunate to be picked up safely.

The following month the squadron lost another aircraft when Flight Sergeant White became disorientated and lost control while flying in cloud. He too baled out safely and was subsequently rescued uninjured.

A rarity on the base was the assembly of a General Field Court Marshal to deal with an Aircraftman who had been charged with stealing a bottle of gin from the NAAFI. He was found guilty and sentenced to six months detention.

No. 684 Mosquito Squadron's detachment were due to arrive on the islands in June and to assist them in the move, four Catalina flying boats of No. 240 Squadron were detailed to fly from their base at Redhills Lake near Madras to the Hoogly River near Calcutta, which was the nearest that the flying boats could get to No 684's base at Alipore and there to collect a number of ground crew and a quantity of equipment and fly them to the Cocos Islands.

Leading Aircraftman Peter Collett, an airframe fitter, was one of the 15 ground staff to be moved and he has good cause to remember his posting to the Cocos Islands in 1945. He joined Catalina JX.435 for the first stage of the flight, which was to be to Koggala, Ceylon. They settled into the cramped confines of the aircraft's hull and the heavily laden Catalina commenced it's take-off run. After several miles under full power the aircraft was unable to become airborne and had to return to the loading area where some of the equipment was off-loaded. After an equally long take-off run the second attempt at becoming airborne was successful and they had an uneventful flight on the first leg of their journey, landing at Koggala in the late afternoon.

After a nights rest they took off in the afternoon of the following day. It was not until they were airborne that the passengers were informed of their destination.

Early on the morning of 27th June 1945, after a tiring flight of 17 hours in the noisy all metal aircraft without the benefit of soundproofing, they were given their first glimpse of their new home while the pilot made a slow circuit of the islands.

Peter Byrne, a member of the islands Marine Section, was on the jetty on Direction Island when the Catalina was first heard. As was usual with the arrival of an aircraft, there were many onlookers who noted that the aircraft flew a normal circuit and then turned towards the North, returning on the North to South line of approach to the landing area in the lagoon. At the time the wind was blowing fairly strongly from the Northwest and the tidal flow into the lagoon was from the Southeast, causing waves which were three to four feet between the crests.

The wind direction and the tidal flow were normal at that location but there was no windsock as is usual on a land runway. There were a number of vessels at anchor to the West of the aircraft's line of approach, all with their bows facing into the wind.

The nearest vessel to the aircraft's flight path was a cable ship and this was anchored by it's stern, which is normal for this type of craft. As the Catalina commenced it's descent, passing between Horsburgh and Direction Islands, it was realised by the onlookers that IT WAS FLYING DOWN WIND.

The hull was seen to touch the water near the commencement of the channel and then bounced high into the air. On it's descent the nose went under the surface in an explosion of white water and spray. The aircraft did not capsize immediately but settled on the water with dense black smoke pouring from the front section. It remained afloat for several minutes, which allowed the watching members of the Marine Section to get small craft to the scene and pull out several of the aircraft's occupants, despite the hazard of smoke and roaring flames.

Of the fourteen men who were on board the flying boat, only seven were rescued alive and two of these died within a few hours. Those who died in this accident were:

Warrant Officer Eric John Freeman, Captain and First Pilot.

Pilot Officer Francis Arthur Marshall, RCAF, 2nd Pilot.

Flight Sergeant Edward William George Denmark,
Wireless Operator/Air Gunner.

Flight Sergeant David James John Paramore,
Navigator/Bomb Aimer.

Flight Sergeant Eric George Spearing,
Wireless Operator/Air Gunner.

The two men of No. 684 Squadron's ground crew
who were killed were:
Corporal Frederick Hawarth – Fitter IIE
Leading Aircraftman Eric John Butler – Photographer.

The survivors, who all received injuries, were given first aid
treatment at the Air/Sea Rescue base and were later removed to
No. 86 Indian General Hospital on West Island. They were:

Warrant Officer Edwin Sinclair Allen, Flight Engineer;

Sergeant James Niven Mitchell, Air Gunner;

Flight Sergeant Robert Edward Short,
Flight Mechanic /Engineer/Air Gunner.

Leading Aircraftman Peter Harry Stanley Collett, Fitter IIA;

Leading Aircraftman William Joseph Liverton, Fitter IIE.

Peter Collett counts himself among the more fortunate in being
only slightly injured. He remembers that after the first hard bump,
he grabbed hold of a protrusion on the bulkhead so tightly that
he cut his fingers to the bone. He then found himself in the water,
clear of the aircraft and suffering from cuts and some broken ribs,
but has no recollection as to how he got there.

On being admitted to the base hospital he was detained for
three weeks before being released to join up with the rest of the
No. 684 Squadron's Detachment having lost all of his kit.

It was not until 1991 that Peter Collett met up with one of his
rescuers, Peter Byrne of the Cocos Islands Air/Sea Rescue base,
and heard from first hand the details of the Catalina's crash.

At the Court of Inquiry, as the facts concerning this tragic
accident became known, some fairly accurate assumptions were
presumed. The pilot of every aircraft has the ultimate responsibility in everything pertaining to the safety of that aircraft and

the pilot of a flying boat has the additional responsibility of anticipating the force and direction of the wind, the height of the waves and the direction of any tidal flow from his observations and any physical sources available. There was no wireless communications to assist the flying boat pilot as to wind or tide direction and, seeing the cable ship at anchor in a perfectly normal manner, he may have based his decision to land in a south easterly direction on the assumption that the vessel was anchored facing into the wind. If that was so, it could well have been the deciding factor in this tragic accident.

The RAF form 1180 (accident record card) shows that Warrant Officer Freeman had accrued 1126 flying hours, 1030 of them on Catalina flying boats. "The conclusion of the Court of Inquiry was that 'In attempting to land downwind on rough seas the pilot was adjudged guilty of negligence' A sad ending to the life of a young man who had served his Country and Squadron well.

Flight Sergeant Sims and Flight Sergeant Benn, together with the two ground staff, Corporal Hawarth and Leading Aircraftman Butler, were buried on the islands until in 1946, when the Royal Air Force evacuated the islands, their remains were exhumed and taken to the War Graves Cemetery at Kranji, Singapore, where their final resting place was among 25,000 other war dead.

For many years the Catalina remained in it's watery grave, 30 feet below the surface of the water in the lagoon. In 1986, Peter Byrne returned to the islands on more pleasant pursuits than those of 1945 and with one of the islands old Marine Pilots made many unsuccessful dives in an endeavour to locate the wreckage. In 1990 a party of Australian divers located and photographed the two engines and the tail, which were found some distance from where the Catalina was known to have sunk. Although the lagoon has a minimal tidal flow, it was discovered that some years earlier, about 1975, there had been reports of a large tidal movement in that part of the Indian Ocean and for a period strong tides had destroyed a great deal of coral and moved many of the wrecks which were known to have lain in the lagoon undisturbed for many years. This probably accounts for the fact that Peter Byrne was unable to locate the wreck of the flying boat at it's last known location.

The day following the accident, the Allied Air Commander-in-Chief, Air Marshal Sir Keith Park, KCB, KBE, MC, DFC, accompanied by Lady Park, arrived on the islands by Sunderland flying boat to carry out an inspection of the new base. One of his first duties was a visit to the Island's hospital to see the injured from the previous days crash.

During his two day visit, Air Marshal Park visited most of the various Army and Air Force units throughout the islands. On his return to India he sent the following signal to the Fortress Commander:

"You and your team have created the best organised base that I have seen in any overseas theatre of war. These results could have been obtained only by the closest cooperation between all three Services and the local Civil Authorities. The air base you are creating will be used shortly as a springboard from which we shall launch an attack against Japanese shipping and bases. Every man who does his job well in our Command is contributing towards winning the war in the Far East. Good Luck to you all".

The Fortress Commander's Standing Orders for the defence of the islands in the event of a Japanese attack were comprehensive and laid down instructions as to what and when action was to be taken. It gave three states of readiness:

State III Codeword 'Clunies', meaning attack not expected.

State II Codeword 'Ross', meaning ground attack probably in 12 hours.

State I. Codeword 'Emden', meaning attack imminent.

During the month of June No. 129 Staging Post had dealt with 50 incoming transit aircraft and had dispatched 49. Food and accommodation had been provided for 408 passengers and they had received 15,629 lbs of incoming freight and had dispatched 2,391 lbs. They had also dealt with 4,884 lbs of incoming mail and sent off 2,903 lbs. With mail arriving twice weekly by flying boat morale amongst the troops was high.

The number of aircraft in transit that were dealt with over the following months rapidly increased but because of the progress of the war in the Far East they at no time approached the figure of 500 multi-engined aircraft a month that the Staging Post had been intended to deal with.

The following is an excerpt from a leaflet which the Royal Air Force Transport Command circulated to passengers on the Ceylon to Australia route to prepare them for their overnight stop at the little known Cocos Islands. It then gives a brief historical note about the islands.

COCOS ISLANDS (Indian Ocean)

Local time GMT 6½

SITE: Group of islands, about a dozen sizable ones, situated some 700 miles SW of Sumatra and 530 miles WSW of Christmas Island. Airfield is on West Island, the largest in the group.

CURRENCY: There is no local money but Indian and Ceylon rupees and Australian currency can be used.

ACCOMMODATION: All tented camp, well situated, clean and comfortable. Service and attention is reported to be exceptional.

FOOD AND DRINK: Food is mainly tinned but there is a good variety and plenty of it. Supplies of liquor are also said to be varied and adequate. N.B. Whenever practicable visiting aircraft should take as much fresh fruit and vegetables as possible. Nothing but coconut palms grow on the islands.

RECREATION: Plenty of bathing and fishing under ideal conditions, no other facilities are available except those organised by the camp members themselves. Nevertheless the spirit and general morale of all is described as exceptional.

TRANSPORT: Only Jeeps on West Island.

CHAPTER 10

Mosquito PRU Operations

THE DETACHMENT of No. 684 Squadron comprised seven Mark 34 PR Mosquitoes fitted with two Merlin 114 two stage engines. With no armour plating or tank bullet proofing, they were capable of a very high speed and were ideal for carrying out very long range photographic reconnaissance missions.

The first operation to be carried out by the detachment from the Cocos Islands was on 2nd July 1945 when the Commanding Officer, Wing Commander Lowry, DFC and his navigator, Flight Sergeant Pateman, took off in Mosquito RC.185 'Z' for a photographic reconnaissance of the Port Swettenham area of Malaya. Meeting no opposition they made 13 runs over the target areas from Morib Point to Pinto Gedong before making similar runs over the airfields of Fort de Kock, Loer and Oekaloeng. On the return flight over the island of Sumatra they made runs over the town and harbour of Emmerhaven where two 150 ft long ships were seen.

The following day Squadron Leader K.J. Newman DFC and Bar and Warrant Officer R.K. Smith, DFM returned to the same areas in aircraft BG.186 'G' and made seven runs over the target area at heights of 25,000 and 29,000 feet. Returning over Boengoer Bay they saw a 300ft merchant ship at anchor.

From these first operations the aircrews flew photographic missions almost every day until the end of hostilities in the Far East, covering the Malayan Peninsular from Penang to Singapore and down the length of Sumatra and Java, gleaning details of roads, railways, harbours, airfields, supply dumps and eventually locating prisoner of war and civilian internment camps.

The flights were made at heights of 30,000ft down to a few hundred feet. On occasions the unarmed aircraft attracted anti-aircraft fire, particularly over the dock area of Singapore but they seldom saw any Japanese fighter aircraft.

The biggest problem that the crews encountered on these very long flights, much of it over the ocean, was the unpredictable weather. Often cloud conditions over the targets made the taking of clear photographs very difficult and violent storms on passage made flying both tiring and dangerous.

On completion of a mission there was initially a delay in obtaining the results of their efforts as the film had to be flown to Ceylon for developing and interpretation. This was overcome when additional staff were brought to the islands and film could be processed on the base.

Much of the developed film was sent to the planners at ACSEA, where preparations were well under way for the recapture of Malaya and the islands of the East Indies (Operations 'Zipper' and 'Mailfist') which were scheduled to take place in the Autumn.

The following entries from the Squadron's daily log shows the extent of the sorties carried out by the Mosquito crews during the month of July 1945.

On the 5th July 1945, Flight Lieutenant Edwards and Warrant Officer C.G. Taylor were briefed to take Mosquito RG.185 'Z' and reconnoitre the road from Kukuo on the Malayan coast as far as Kuala Lumpur. This part of the flight was only partially successful due to there being 5/10th cloud and also intercom failure. However they had more success in taking shots of the road from Kukup to Semarah, Kualar Lumpur to Port Swettenham. Port Dickinson to Telok-Datok (Morib) and from Malacca to Alorgajah. On the 6th, Flight Lieutenant D.D. Warwick and Flying Officer G.H. Jones took Mosquito RG.184 'X' to the same areas where they found conditions to be still very cloudy. They photographed the harbour at Port Dickinson and the airfield and town of Morib. A new airstrip was seen to be under construction on the airfield at

Pakanbaroe and an enemy aircraft was seen to take off and fly in an easterly direction, apparently having no interest in the high flying mosquito.

On the 7th, the Commanding Officer and Flight Sergeant Jones took off for the long flight to Singapore but had to abort the mission due to cloud and a Memver front stretching over the whole of Sumatra.

On the 11th Flight Lieutenant Warwick and Flying Officer Jones were again off to the Malayan Peninsular in aircraft RG.187 'H', photographing roads from Morib to Port Dickinson and on to Malacca, at a height of 14,000 feet. In the harbour at Port Dickinson they noted eight 90ft coasters and a further four in Malacca harbour.

On the 12th, Wing Commander Lowry and Flight Sergeant Pateman carried out a successful sortie in Mosquito RG.186 'G', to photograph the airfields at Changi, Yio Chukand, Seleter, Sembawan and Kual from a height of 30,000 feet. Shipping in the Naval, Commercial and Engraving Docks at Singapore and the railway line from Kulai to Johore was also photographed. In the Singapore Naval Dock, two large ships, possibly battleships and three others, possibly cruisers were seen. Three motor vessels were seen off Port Seleter and five more at Buonavista. Eight more vessels were seen in Keppel harbour.

While over the Singapore dock area they attracted 30 bursts of heavy anti aircraft fire but it was well below the height of their aircraft.

On the 13th, Squadron Leader Newman and Warrant Officer Smith went to the Port Swettenham area in aircraft RG.187 'H' where they made twelve runs over the airfields at Emmerhaven, Padang and Morib. A further, seven runs were made over Port Swettenham and Klang. At Emmerhaven they saw two 400ft motor vessels and at Morib four 150ft and seven 90ft coasters. While over Morib, an enemy aircraft was seen flying on a south easterly course and at Padang a twin engined Japanese aircraft was seen to take off.

On the 14th, Flight Lieutenant Edwards and Warrant Officer Taylor took off in RG.191 'M' to cover the beaches and airfields in the Morib area. When they were 450 miles from base and at a height of 20,000 feet, they experienced violent 'blower surges' and both engines cut out. A lot of height was lost before they could re-start the engines and then only the starboard one would function correctly. The vibrations from the port engine were so violent that it was shut down and the propeller was feathered. The wing tanks were jettisoned but height could not be maintained until they were down to 100 feet above the waves. When the base came into sight they made a direct approach but were unable to complete the final 600 feet to the airstrip and undershot into the bay. Neither man was injured but the aircraft was a 'write off' and was later broken up.

Flight Lieutenant Warwick and Flying Officer Jones were also airborne that day in Mosquito RG.184 'X' and flew to Malaya where they covered the airfields at Malacca, Batupatah and Muar town and then Malacca Port and the whole of the coastline to Kukup.

On the 16th, Wing Commander Lowry and Flight Sergeant Pateman in RG.186 'G' covered the roads in the Kuala Lumpur area but clouds at 25,000 feet prevented them visiting other targets.

The 17th saw Squadron Leader Newman and Warrant Officer Smith airborne in RG.185 'Z' and they spent seventy minutes over Singapore Island at 30,000 feet, covering the airfields at Changi, Seleter, Sembawan and JohoreBaru and the two coastal strips from Buonavista to Pulai-Brani and Pulai-Brani down the coast to the east of Singapore town. Two runs were also made over the Naval Docks in Singapore harbour where five Naval craft, including possibly two cruisers were seen and five motor vessels of some 400 feet were also seen in the Commercial Docks. One enemy aircraft was seen to take off from the airfield at Changi.

On 21st the same two Officers took RG.187 'H' to cover the airfields at Batu Pahat, Kluang, Kulaisara, Labis, Muir and Benut from a height of 14,000 feet. Two enemy aircraft were seen to the south-east of Kluang airfield. On setting course for the return to base they climbed to 26,000 feet and when 650 miles from the Cocos Islands the starboard engine became u/s and had to be feathered. They were able to maintain a height of 16,000 feet on the remaining engine and landed safely.

On the 22nd, the airfields at Benut, Batu Pahat, Yong, Peng and Kluang were covered by Flight Lieutenant Warwick and Flying Officer Jones in RG.186 'G'. They also covered the roads from Batu Pahat to Kluang. Included in their targets were factories in the airfield areas near Yong Peng and the town of Paloh The runs were mostly made at heights of 10,000 feet but for some they came down to 6,000 and 3,000 feet.

On the 25th, Flight Lieutenant Andrews and Warrant Officer Painter in RG.185 'Z' carried out their first operation from the Cocos Islands and visited the Malayan Peninsula, covering the road from Segamat to Yong Peng at 17,000 feet. Other targets at Ula Tiram and Singapore Island were covered at 10,000 feet. An enemy cruiser was seen in the Naval Dockyard at Singapore and three 3,000 ton motor vessels were seen in the Johore Straits. Five enemy aircraft were seen at Tebrua and on the return flight photographs were taken of Standing Island.

Another new crew, Flight Lieutenant H.G. Sambrook and Flight Lieutenant Garnet covered the Port Dickinson area and the airfields at Kajang, Uly Bernan and Kerling in RG.185 'G' the same day.

On the 26th, Squadron Leader Newman and Flight Sergeant Pateman took RG.184 'X' to Segamat Sacil and Singapore Island. Their patrol was at a height of 30,000 feet and they saw two possible cruisers, a possible destroyer and one 400 foot motor vessel in the Johore Straits.

On the 27th, Flight Lieutenant Warwick and Flying Officer Jones took RG.185 'Z' to the Serang River and Kuala Lumpur areas, covering Port Swettenham and the docks at Port Dickinson where six coastal vessels were seen.

On the 28th, Flight Lieutenant Andrews and Warrant Officer Painter followed up the sorties of the previous day, by taking

RG.186 'G' back to the Serang River and Kuala Lumpur areas. On the outward flight they photographed a 350 foot motor vessel in Boengoes Bay and also visited Padang. The main targets of Sepang and Port Swettenham were photographed at heights of 30,000 and 25,000 feet.

On the 29th, Flight Lieutenant Sambrook and Flight Lieutenant Garnet flying in RG.203 'E' met adverse weather conditions and after photographing the beaches at K.G. Chuah Morib from 15,000 feet had to abort the rest of the mission.

Squadron Leader Newman and Warrant Officer Smith returned to these beaches the following day in RG 'X' and also visited the airfields at Batu Pahat and photographed the road from Muar to Segamat, the beaches from Morib to K.G. Tembok and the coast road at Senggararang at 6,000 feet and 16,000 feet. Nine 90ft coastal vessels were seen at Port Dickinson.

Since their first mission on 2nd July 1945, the seven aircraft of No. 684 Squadron's detachment on the Cocos Islands had carried out 27 successful photographic reconnaissance missions to Malaya, Java and Sumatra almost every day. One was aborted due to bad weather and one aborted because of mechanical failure.

It was as a result of the photographs taken by these aircrews that future air strikes were planned and were also the means from which information vital to the planning of operations for the re-occupation of Japanese held territory were obtained. An essential part of these operations was to search and locate the many prisoner of war and civilian internment camps, very often deep in the jungles of the occupied territories. When the war was finally over, many of these camps continued to be under the control of the Japanese for many weeks prior to the arrival of Allied troops. For several days after the Emperor of Japan had accepted the Allied terms of surrender the unarmed Mosquitos continued to attract antiaircraft fire, particularly over the Singapore Docks area.

The longest distance flown by a Mosquito aircraft operating from the Cocos Islands was made on 20th August 1945, when Flight Lieutenant Manners and Warrant Officer Burley, flying in aircraft 'J', flew to Penang Island off the north coast of Malaya, a distance of 1,240 miles. Adding the miles flown while carrying out their photographic mission the round trip covered 2,600 miles in a flying time of 9 hours 5 minutes.

In August a further 22 missions were carried out during which 9,460 operational and 2,909 non operational exposures were taken. These flights continued until 25th September when all further photographic reconnaissance operations were cancelled and the detachment prepared to rejoin the parent Squadron.

In six weeks of actual wartime operations from the Cocos Islands the aircrews of No. 684 Squadron's detachment had flown 38 operations over Malaya, Java and Sumatra. By the end of the year No. 684 Squadron was to become the principal Photographic Reconnaissance Unit in the Far East.

The 31st August 1945 was probably the most memorable in the lives of Flight Lieutenant C.G. Andrews, RNZAF and his navigator, Warrant Officer Painter. It was also a major entry in No. 684 Squadron's record book and a minor event in the history of World War 2 when, due to a malfunctioning engine on their Mosquito RG.210 'J', they became the first Allied aircraft to land on the airfield at Kallang, Singapore, since it had been occupied by the Japanese in 1942.

Engine failure in an aircraft is always a very worrying factor, especially when the aircraft is on a flight over hundreds of miles of sea, but that thought was not in the minds of the two crew members as they received their briefing to carry out a reconnaissance flight to Singapore Island and obtain photographs of the airfield at Kallang from a height of 5,000 feet. They took off from the Cocos Islands at 0610 hours and crossed the mountains of Sumatra at 20,000 feet. When they were within one hours flying time of their target they commenced a slow descent. As they did so, Flight Lieutenant Andrews noticed that the revs of the starboard engine had dropped from 2300 to 2200 but he was unable to rectify the fault. On a Mosquito aircraft the starboard engine supplies the power to the main batteries and they in turn provide the power to operate the various instruments and navigational aids.

As experienced airmen, both crew members knew that there was no question of trying to cross the mountains of Sumatra followed by the long sea crossing back to base with insufficient power in the aircraft's batteries. They were also aware that there was bad weather en-route. The only option open to them was to attempt a landing at Kallang airfield – the very airfield that would have been the object of their mission.

It was a most frightening decision to have to make as the airfield and surrounding area was still occupied by Japanese Forces whose reaction to their arrival was unpredictable. His Imperial Highness the Emperor of Japan had agreed that his Forces were to cease hostilities over two weeks earlier but Japanese anti-aircraft guns on Singapore Island were still firing at Allied aircraft and there were many Japanese units that had not known defeat in the field and were still in occupation of much of the territory they had gained in 1941/2.

The Japanese were not known for their charitable treatment of those who fell into their hands, particularly aircrew, who were the subject of a Japanese High Command's order instructing that they were to be executed. Only a few weeks earlier, on the 7th July 1945, ten Australian soldiers were beheaded for their part in attempting to carry out a raid on Japanese naval ships in Singapore harbour in December 1943.

Having made the decision to land at Kallang airfield, Flight Lieutenant Andrews made a quick circuit of the airfield and lined up the Mosquito to make a perfect landing on the 1800 feet of concrete runway. On reaching the end of his landing run, Japanese ground staff appeared and marshalled him to a parking area, the same as would be expected by any visiting aircraft.

With some trepidation the two airmen climbed stiffly from the Mosquito and approached a line of Japanese Officers. Initially there was a language difficulty but this was resolved when a Japanese Air Force Officer, a Staff Officer and an interpreter arrived from Singapore City. Apparently the Officers had been expecting a Dakota aircraft to arrive with a contingent of officers from Lord Louis Mountbatten's Headquarters to finalise the terms of surrender for the Japanese troops on Singapore Island.

The Japanese showed great courtesy to both the British airmen who were eventually taken to a prisoner of war camp at Changi for the night where they met other RAF men and arranged to have their Mosquito repaired the following morning. Before leaving the airfield the Japanese posted a guard on the aircraft and a No. 356 Squadron Liberator from their own base was seen to make several passes over the airfield, apparently having noted the Mosquito.

The following morning they returned to the Mosquito with an RAF Fitter and Rigger and the fault in the aircraft's engine was soon located and repaired. While the repair was being carried out, Squadron Leader Newman, the Commanding Officer of No. 684 Squadron's detachment, arrived in another aircraft and in due course the two Mosquitos returned to the Cocos Islands together.

A few hours after the Mosquito went missing the author, who was not aware that an aircraft was missing, was working in the signals workshop at Station HQ on the Cocos Islands where a portable radio was always tuned in to Radio SEAC, the Forces radio programme broadcasting from Ceylon, when over the music a very powerful male voice was heard repeating in English, 'This is the Japanese Army Command Headquarters, Singapore calling Lord Louis Mountbatten, the Supreme Commander South East Asia Command, India. Today one of your Mosquito aircraft landed at Kallang Airfield, Singapore and the crew, Flight Lieutenant Andrews and Warrant Officer Painter are safe'.

A telephone call to a colleague in Flying Control revealed that one of No. 684 detachment's Mosquitoes, crewed by the two named airmen had indeed been reported as being overdue from an operation in the Singapore area.

The report of the broadcast was received with great delight by the members of No. 684 Squadron's detachment and the following day Squadron Leader Newman flew to Kallang, returning in the company of the missing Mosquito and its crew.

On their safe return Flight Lieutenant Andrews and Squadron Leader Newman were each required to submit the following reports for the information of the Fortress Commander.

To The Air Officer Commanding RAF Cocos Islands.
From; Flight Lieutenant C.G. Andrews, RNZAF,
No. 684 Squadron Detachment, Cocos Islands.

3rd September 1945.

Subject; Forced landing at Kallang Airfield
of Mosquito 'J', crew F/Lt Andrews. W/O Painter.

Sir,
I have the honour to report, that on August 31st 1945, at 0610 hours, I took off from Cocos Islands with my navigator, Warrant Officer Painter, to carry out a sortie in the Singapore area to obtain photographs of Kallang Airfield. The photos were to be taken at a low altitude, so one hour from my E.T.A. I descended from 20,000 ft to 5,000 ft. 20 minutes from the target I noticed that the starboard engine revs had dropped from 2300 to 2200. I attempted to re-synchronise but was unable to do so as using the pitch control made no difference. I inspected the linkage of the pitch control inside the cockpit and it appeared to be alright so it must have been a failure of the linkage of the engine mounted controls or failure of the control attached to the constant speed unit.
The revs fell to 1900 and twice before I have had similar experiences and knew that I would be unable to get sufficient power from the starboard engine to allow sufficient power to climb over the Sumatra mountains. High frontal clouds, bad weather plus low revs on the starboard engine would not be enough to give power for the generator to charge the batteries, so radio aid, essential part of navigation, would be useless.
I decided, with some trepidation, to land at Kallang Airfield, Singapore Island, which had a 1800 foot concrete runway. We landed at 10.20 hours and the Japanese marshalled us to a parking

area the other side of the airfield. I tried to tell the Japanese that the aircraft was u/s but couldn't make them understand. Eventually an interpreter arrived and then a Japanese Air Force Officer and a Staff Officer from Singapore.

Great courtesy was shown by the Japanese who offered to broadcast over Singapore Radio my whereabouts and the reason for landing. I was asked if I intended to take off that day and said "Yes, if the trouble could be located". Eventually some tools were produced and three Japanese helped us to take the engine cover off and locate the trouble. The engine was still too hot to work on (the repairs were eventually carried out by a POW Fitter from a nearby camp the following day).

I told the Japanese that there was insufficient time to carry out the repairs that day and they offered me accommodation at the Raffles Hotel. I declined when I learned that I could contact two Army Officers who had parachuted in the previous day to Changi. I was given some food and a Liberator flew over the airfield and made several passes on seeing the Mosquito. I was unable to attract it's attention.

I was taken to a POW camp at Changi where I contacted Lt. Wishard who had landed by parachute and was organising supply drops for the POWs. The Japanese provided a guard for the aircraft and were threatened with their lives if anything happened to the aircraft. The only question of a military nature that I was asked was what the top speed of the Mosquito was. I said that I had never tried.

I met Wing Commander Wills-Sandford, the Senior Air Force Officer in the camp who arranged for an Engineering Officer, Fitter and Rigger to carry out repairs to my aircraft. I left the camp the next day with Flight Lieutenant Sturrocks, a Fitter and a Rigger and Major Wills, who acted as interpreter, and a Japanese Officer as hostage. The repairs were carried out and the engine was tested. The revs remained constant.

While working on the aircraft, Mosquito 'E' appeared overhead and flew low several times across the field. I gave the OK sign and shortly afterwards the aircraft landed. The Japanese ground crew *again marshalled the aircraft. We were indeed relieved to meet the crew, S/Ldr Newman and P/O Burns and learned that they had heard of our whereabouts from the Jap. radio and a Liberator. S/Ldr Newman had expected R/T communication with me while flying overhead but as my batteries were fairly low I dared not use them more for fear of not being able to start my engines.*

S/Ldr Newman and I inspected the runway with a view to it's capabilities and made the decision that it was suitable for heavy aircraft of the Liberator standard. Lunch was again supplied by the Japs. We took off at 12.50 hrs. and set course for base. I used the Jap fuel en-route at low cruising power. It operated satisfactorily. Touch down at base was 16.20 hrs.

I have the honour to be, Sir,
Your obedient Servant,
C.G. Andrews.

Report of Squadron Leader K.J. Newman.

Sir,

Subject - Landing at Singapore.

1. I have the honour to report that on the 1st September 1945 at 0620 hours, I took off in Mosquito 'E' for a P.R. sortie and search for Flt/Lt Andrews, (Mosquito 'J') who had not returned from a sortie on the 31st August 1945.

2. Probable position of aircraft 'J' was known from reports intercepted from Japanese controlled radio in Singapore, which stated that a twin engined aircraft force landed at Kallang airfield at approximately 1200 hrs on the 31st August 1945. Also reported from a 356 Liberator after crew reported seeing a Mosquito in dispersals at Kallang airfield in the afternoon of the 31st.

3. I arrived at Kallang airfield at 1000 hours and sighted a P.R. Mosquito on the grass. I circled several times very low, during which times I tried to contact the aircraft on VHF, with no success. I saw what I thought to be Europeans working on the aircraft and also saw several Europeans in company of Flt/Lt Andrews. I received a visual OK signal from Flt/Lt/ Andrews and decided to land to determine;

(1) Cause of forced landing.

(2) Extent of damage caused by forced landing, if any.

(3) What steps had been taken to repair the trouble and/or if any extra equipment or spares were needed to make the aircraft serviceable.

4. On enquiry after landing I found that there was an Engineering Officer, Fitter and Rigger from the POW camp on the Job. After a chat with Flt/Lt Andrews and Flt/Lt. Storrock (EO) I learned that temporary repairs were being carried out and that in the opinion of the Engineering Officer the aircraft would be serviceable for the return trip to base. I witnessed the engine being run up, the pitch control was found operating satisfactorily.

5. Within 15 minutes of my landing a Japanese Staff car appeared complete with Staff Major and Stooge. I was introduced amid much bowing and saluting etc, by Major Wild* from the POW camp, who acted as interpreter. Major Wild proved most helpful during my stay.

6. The Japanese were most polite and helpful and could not do enough for us. They supplied an excellent lunch which was most

---

Major Cyril Wild is the subject of another book published by Woodfield. *Cyril Wild: The Tall Man Who Never Slept* by James Bradley tells the extraordinary story of this British Army Major who was fluent in Japanese and played an important role as interpreter at the surrender of Singapore to the Japanese in 1941 and again in 1945 when the Japanese surrendered to the Allies. In between these events he was a prisoner of war of the Japanese and suffered the privations of life in the labour camps along the banks of the river Kwai where allied POWs endured squalid conditions as they worked to build the infamous 'death railway' between Burma and Thailand. During these years Wild put his knowledge of Japanese to good use and is remembered fondly by many former POWs who benefited greatly from his negotiating skills.

enjoyable. I refused an offer to return with the Jap. Major to his mess for lunch. They also supplied us with fuel reported to be 100 octane. This was put in the bomb bay tank and was to be used if necessary and then only at cruising conditions. Refuelling was carried out by the Japanese ground staff.

7. I inspected the runway with Flt/Lt. Andrews and decided that as it was concrete and appeared in good condition, was suitable for heavy aircraft. Length was 1850 yds x 50 yds. The Jap. interpreter informed me that they were evacuating both Kallang and Changi area and airfields as they were for use by the British. He also informed me that Changi airfield was approximately 2500 yds x 100 yds. but was not surfaced and would be of use for heavy aircraft only in fair weather.

I took off at 1250 hrs and landed at base at 1620 hrs after an uneventful trip. As cloud base was low no photos were taken.

I have the honour to be, Sir,
Your Obedient Servant,
K.J. Newman. S/L.

On the day that the Mosquitos carried out their first operation from the Cocos Islands, an ENSA (Entertainment National Service Association) party arrived on the base, giving a welcome break to the routine of hard work. This group was 'Waldini's Gipsy Band' and a supporting cast. As the band comprised two men and eight girls, they received a stupendous welcome wherever they went on the islands from the thousands of men who had been starved of female company for months and in some cases years.

If any female was due to arrive on any of the many transport aircraft passing through the Staging Post, a notice would appear in Daily Routing Orders requiring all ranks wear shorts or trousers and to be decently clothed. The order would be rescinded as soon as the female(s) had departed. The reason for the order was that in the all male environment that existed on the base, the men wore the minimum of clothing when working and on the domestic sites this would very often be no more than a towel around the waist.

The first Dakota aircraft to pass through the Staging Post arrived on the 8th July and damaged an airscrew on landing. When the aircraft was air tested some of the ground staff had the opportunity to see the islands from the air.

On the 9th July at 0902 hours the Radar picked up a hostile aircraft 40 miles South-East of the base at an estimated 3000ft. It was plotted to 75 miles North-East and was then believed to have climbed away. At that time only the MRU 'A' system was available which was unable to give an accurate estimate of heights. A section of Spitfires was airborne at the time and was vectored on to the hostile aircraft but no interception was made. A second section was scrambled when the track was picked up at 12 miles North but they could not overtake the target and did not see it.

On 12th July, two Army Officers of Force 136, Major Deeming and Lieutenant Knight-Hall, arrived and established a small Headquarters to liaison with No. 99 Squadron and No. 175 Wing in the SD operations over Malaya. The keeping of the clandestine Forces supplied was considered essential as they were to be a vital link in the forthcoming offensive in Malaya.

A very welcome arrival was a ship carrying fresh meat, fruit and vegetables. This was the first to arrive since the landings had been made and as none of the Units had refrigeration every mess and cookhouse throughout the islands kept open house in order to use the produce before it went bad.

Liberators lined up on the runway of the Cocos Islands air base, 1944.

CHAPTER 11

Liberator Shipping Strikes

ON 2ND JULY THE FIRST OF THE Long Range General Reconnaissance (LRGR) aircraft and their ground staff commenced to
arrive. The first was a party of ground staff of No. 321 (Dutch)
Squadron, comprising 72 mixed Dutch and British Other Ranks
under a Dutch Officer. They were met by Lieutenant H.M. Karson,
the Squadron's Engineering Officer, who had arrived a few days
earlier and, with the willing assistance of the men of No. 129
Staging Post, had prepared tented accommodation for them.

The advance party were soon followed by the detachment's six
Liberator bombers and two Amphibious Catalina flying boats
(Canso) under the command of Lieutenant Commander de
Bruyn, Royal Netherlands Naval Air Service. The flying boats, two
of the 570 Catalinas supplied to the Royal Air Force by America
during World War II, were under the command of Lieutenant
Commander Aerant. They were to be land based and used for air/
sea rescue patrols whenever the bombers were operating.

No. 321 Squadron was one of three Dutch Squadrons serving
with the Royal Air Force. Both of the other squadrons were based
in the United Kingdon; one, No. 322 was equipped with Spitfires
and the other, No. 320, was equipped with Mitchell medium
bombers. During its four years of service with the RAF, No. 321
Squadron had suffered only one fatal flying accident. This
occurred when one of it's Liberators was taking off from the main
base at China Bay, Ceylon, and crashed, killing all those on board.

To operate with No. 321 Squadron's detachment a detachment
of No. 203 Squadron (RAF) also arrived on the islands from their

main base at Kankesanturia, Ceylon, under the command of Squadron Leader Fletcher. Other aircraft of this squadron also commenced to make regular visits carrying passengers and freight.

During July the operations and administrative control of RAF Station Cocos Islands was transferred from ACSEA to No. 222 Group and that of No. 129 Staging Post to HQ No. 229 Group.

On 15th July No. 321 Squadron's detachment carried out its first operation from the Cocos Islands when Lieutenant Commander de Bruyn in Liberator 'Y' and Lieutenant Hofelt in 'V' were sent on an armed reconnaissance to the Sunda Straits between Java and Sumatra.

In good weather and with visibility of some 15 miles the two aircraft had uneventful flights which lasted 10 hours 20 minutes. During the course of these patrols Lieutenant Commander Aerant carried out an air/sea rescue patrol in the slow flying Canso 'J' along the known track of the two Liberators.

On 22nd July Lieutenant Commander de Bruyn was again airborne in the same aircraft to report on the movements of a 4,000 ton motor vessel which had previously been seen in the Port of Emmerhaven. At Tandjoeng Point they saw and attacked an observation post with machine gun fire and bombed a small beached sailing vessel with eight 250 lb GP (General Purpose) bombs, causing some damage from near misses. Six other vessels were sighted during the 14 hour 14 minute patrol.

The same day, Flying Officer Webster of No. 203 Squadron was detailed to take Liberator 'P' on an anti-shipping patrol from Padang, Sumatra to the Sunda Straits. On reaching his patrol area he sighted the 4,000 ton vessel that had previously been reported on and saw that it had moved about one mile to the south of Emmerhaven Port and 'under the shelter of the hills bordering Boengoes Bay. Turning in a wide sweep he attacked the ship from 100 feet, scoring three hits. There was no return fire. On resuming his patrol he saw a convoy of six small coastal craft being escorted by a small Japanese warship.

Two days later, Flight Lieutenant MacDonald in Liberator 'H' of No. 203 Squadron, Lieutenants Wanroot and Petschi in No. 321 Squadron's 'M' and 'Z' returned to the attack. The vessel was still in Boengoes Bay and the aircraft made individual attacks. Flight Lieutenant MacDonald carried out two low level passes and each time his bombs failed to release, his gunners swept the super-structure of the ship with machine gun fire on each pass. He then stood off to let the Dutch aircraft make their attacks. Lieutenant Wanroot dropped eight 250lb GP bombs causing damage with two direct hits and three near misses.

When Lieutenant Petschi made his bombing run his aircraft's bomb-doors failed to open. He pulled away and saw another small coaster and carried out an attack with eight 250lb bombs. On this occasion the bomb doors functioned correctly and the crew of the ship (about 25) were seen to jump overboard into the path of the dropping bombs. During the course of this mission Lieutenant Valk was on air/sea rescue patrol in Canso 'Q'.

On 28th July Squadron Leader Fletcher in 203's 'H, carried out an unarmed reconnaissance patrol of Tjilatjap on the south coast of Java. On an unarmed reconnaissance no bombs were carried but usually some hand held cameras. Low cloud over Tjilatjap harbour reduced visibility but a 300 foot motor vessel and a Japanese naval escort vessel were seen. Further along the coast and about one mile west of the town a number of gun emplace-ments and what appeared to be a prison block were seen and photographed.

On the 30th Lieutenant Commander de Bruyn in 'Y' and Lieutenant Hofelt in 'V' were airborne at 0300 hours on an unarmed reconnaissance patrol of the south Java coast. In Wijnkcops Bay they sighted an enemy patrol vessel accom-panying a wooden barge and in Tjilatjap harbour a single funnel two-masted motor vessel of between 2,000 and 3,000 tons was tied up alongside the quay. There were also two small coasters and several wooden ships apparently under construction nearby and several sunken ships in the outer harbour.

On leaving the coast they passed over Kambangan Island. Noting what appeared to be a guard house they then saw a prison camp about a mile further inland with the inmates waving at the Liberator as it flew overhead. On the beaches many overgrown trenches surrounded by barbed wire were seen and the two aircraft were fired upon from two of four observation posts. Neither aircraft was hit and they landed safely back at base at 1530 hours, a patrol of 12 hours 30 minutes.

The 31st July was another busy day for the islands' Liberators. Lieutenant Petschi in 321 Squadron's 'Z' made an early start and had reached his patrol area by 0645 hours. A visit to Semaneka Bay showed it to be empty of shipping and at Lampoeng Bay only two small sailing boats were seen. At 0743 hours a 120 foot ferry steamer of about 100 tons was seen travelling at about 5 knots. The Liberator made an immediate attack with eight 250lb bombs fitted with 11 second fuses from a height of 50 feet. The aircraft's gunners fired 450 rounds of .5-inch ammunition and as the aircraft climbed away the crew saw the bombs straddle the ship and explode causing it to break into two parts and sink.

Lieutenent Hofelt was also on patrol in the same area in aircraft 'V' when he located a 120 foot long coastal craft which he immediately attacked from 70 feet, dropping eight 250lb GP bombs while his gunners fired 1400 rounds with their .5 inch machine guns. The bombs were seen to straddle the ship which commenced to turn in circles, apparently out of control. While the Dutch aircraft were attacking the ships a Japanese 'Val' aircraft was seen to be shadowing them. It approached Lieutenant Hofelt's 'V' as if to carry out an attack but when the waist and tail gunners commenced to fire in it's direction it immediately turned and flew towards Teloekbetoeng.

A third aircraft of No. 321 Squadron, 'Y' was flown by Lieutenant Commander de Bruyn on an unarmed reconnaissance of the Java Head area and noted a small coastal vessel in the harbour at Merak.

While aircraft of the Dutch squadron were making their successful attacks on the enemy ships Flying Officer Webster and

Flying Officer St John of No. 203 Squadron flew in aircraft 'P' and 'R' on uneventful patrols from Henkoelen to the Sunda Straits.

Many of the men of No. 321 Squadron's detachment had originally come from the islands of the Netherland East Indies and on escaping from the Japanese had been absorbed into the squadron which had been formed in the United Kingdon in 1940. The patrols over Java and Sumatra gave them their first sight of their homeland in three years of danger and hardship, made even harder for some by the knowledge that their loved ones were still imprisoned on the islands and were subject to the oppression of the Japanese.

On 23rd July the base was thrown into confusion when a very high tide poured over the outer reef in the early hours of the morning and some 18" of water swept through the tents on the domestic site at the southern end of West Island. These tents were about four feet above the normal high water mark. Between the barrier reef and the island's beaches was over a quarter of a mile of normally very shallow water and rock pools which almost dried out at low water.

The arrival of the sea through the tents while it was still dark was very frightening and it was very easy to visualise the islands sinking into the depths of the ocean without trace. No doubt that in daylight only the palm trees growing out of the water would have been seen. Fortunately, after the first tremendous surge of water it soon drained away although part of the airstrip remained under water and vehicles had to be parked all over it to hold the pierced steel plating in position. The airstrip was out of commission for 24 hours. Reports from Australia later said that the abnormally high water was the result of a tidal wave in the southern part of the Indian Ocean.

While the detachments of No. 321 and No. 203 Squadrons had commenced to fly on anti shipping operations, two complete heavy bomber squadrons arrived on the base. No. 99 Squadron had a long and distinguished record and was under the command of Wing Commander A. Webster, DFC. and No. 356 Squadron under the command of Wing Commander C.H.B. Sparkes, RCAF.

The later squadron was young in service but with an impressive record of action on the Burma front. Both squadrons were equipped with Liberators and arrived with their Service Echelons (Ground Staff).

In June both squadrons had been withdrawn from operations and the aircrews sent on a course where they were introduced to the technique of supply dropping with and without parachute at very low levels. On completion of the course they returned to their main bases where their postings were announced. At that stage they were not told of their final destination, only that the move was under the code name of 'Bernard'.

Les Parsons, a navigator with No. 99 Squadron had only recently completed a tour of 31 operations on Lancasters of No. 622 Squadron with Bomber Command in Europe. Usually when a crew had competed a tour of operations they were 'screened' for a period of six months. In his case a number of tour expired Lancaster crews were posted to the Far East. On arrival in India they were informed that there was a shortage of experienced heavy bomber crews in South East Asia Command and persuaded that if they wished to stay together as a crew and carry on flying together, they would have to take a conversion course on Liberator aircraft. Most of the crews elected to do this and after the course Les was posted with the rest of his crew to No. 99 Squadron where the seven man Lancaster crews were augmented to eleven by the addition of a second pilot and extra gunners.

On reaching the squadron they carried out a number of operations over the Burma front and then the whole squadron commenced low flying training. Rumours were rife as to the squadron's future role but it was not until the 16th of the month that this started to be revealed to the crews. At 0530 that day the No. 99 Squadron crews were assembled in the briefing room at their base at Dhubalia, some 60 miles from Calcutta. They were informed that the squadron was moving station and the aircraft would be flying some of the ground staff and their equipment to the new station while the rest of the ground staff would travel by boat. The first stage of the flight would be to Kankesanturia on the northern tip of Ceylon where they would get their final briefing.

Taking off at 0705, Les Parsons found that his aircraft was loaded with some of the squadron's kitchen staff and their equipment. They landed at Kankesanturia at 14.45 hours after a very bumpy flight of 7 hours 40 minutes.

The crews had time for a meal before attending their final briefing at 1730 hours. On entering the briefing room all eyes turned to the large covered map on one wall. When all were assembled the map was uncovered and showed large expanses of the Indian Ocean. A thread ran from Kankesanturia and appeared to end in the middle of this Ocean. It was only on closer inspection that the words Cocos/Keeling Islands could be seen on the map at the end of the thread.

The briefing went ahead and they were told that the islands were to be their new base and that in due course they would be informed as to the type of operations they would be undertaking. During the briefing it was emphasised that their outward flight was to be at low level so as to be below a belt of violent thunderstorms that was across their flight path. With few Radar facilities, navigation reverted to basics using astro navigation by the stars when possible. Wireless silence was to be strictly maintained but the crews were delighted when they were informed that the Cocos Islands base would be transmitting bearings from a low powered radio beacon. They considered this to be essential in locating the tiny atolls during the later stages of a flight of nearly 2,000 miles.

Les Parsons' take off time was 1945 hours and they had a tiring but uneventful flight of just over 13 hours, landing at 0855 hours. After the long flight over the sea he says that to see the waves breaking over the outer reef of the islands barely two miles off the port side of the aircraft was a relief, both to him as Navigator and to the rest of the crew.

A hot meal was waiting for them and they were allocated tents in which to settled down and await the main body of airmen who were arriving by sea. They were still unaware as to where the

Squadron fitted in with the few Liberators, Mosquitoes, Spitfires and the Canso that were parked beside the airstrip.

A few days later the aircrew were assembled for a briefing by an Army Officer who informed them of the role that the squadron was to play in forthcoming operations. They were told that although they would still be engaged in bombing operations, their first priority would be the dropping of arms and equipment to Special Forces operating behind the Japanese lines in Southern Malaya, particularly in the Cameron Highlands beyond Kuala Lumpur. These clandestine groups were earmarked to play a vital part when the main Allied Army of Liberation commenced to make seaborne landings later in the year.

The guerrilla units were loosely controlled from the head-quarters of Force 136, based in Ceylon, who maintained regular wireless contact with them but they needed a constant supply of weapons and supplies to keep them effective. Liberator squad-rons in Burma had been dropping airborne supplies to these units but the distances involved meant that the payload was minimal. By using the Cocos Islands as a base the shorter distance to the target areas meant that the aircraft could carry a far greater payload.

Many of the aircrew who were engaged on these type of operations in the Far East have since maintained that they were more frightening and dangerous than normal bombing missions. The missions were usually flown in darkness, often in bad visibility, always at low level with their flight path twisting through mountains and high ground the subject of violent storms where an error in navigation could bring disaster. This was in addition to the normal hazards that could be expected when operating over enemy occupied territory.

The dropping zones (DZs), were given code names such as 'Tideway and 'Funnel' and when the crews commenced these Special Duty (SD) missions they were of 12 to 15 hours duration. Commencing with several hundred miles of low level flying over the sea to avoid alerting the Japanese, they crossed the west coast of Sumatra and climbing over the Barisan Mountain range where the peaks rose to nearly 14,000 feet and then back to low level above green inhospitable forests followed by another sea crossing of the Straits of Malacca before reaching the further hazards of the Highlands of Malaya with their mists, tropical storms and high winds. Having successfully reached the area of the dropping zone they then had to locate accurately the three pinpricks of weak lights marking the spot where they were to drop their supplies. All the hazards then had to be faced again by the weary crews on the return flight. The supply dropping operations took a heavy toll of the aircraft and crews engaged.

On 18th July the squadron had cause to celebrate when it was known that the Commanding Officer, Wing Commander Webster, had been awarded the Distinguished Service Order.

The main party of the squadron's personnel arrived on HMT Dilwara on 30th July and with the squadron at its full strength of 16 Liberators, three crews were briefed to carry out a shipping strike on a 3,000 ton motor vessel which had been located in the harbour at Tjilatjap on the south coast of Java.

F.E. Collier, a fitter/armourer on No. 99 Squadron's ground staff remembers the panic prior to getting the three aircraft bombed up for the mission when it was found that due to their hurried departure from India no bomb release wires had been packed. With the ingenuity that very often has to be practiced by those working under field conditions, packing case wire was substituted. The bombs were brought from the beachhead bomb dump to the waiting aircraft by a narrow gauge railway operated by a small diesel engine.

The squadron's Commanding Officer, Wing Commander Webster, led Flying Officer McLaws and Squadron Leader Alcorn on the operation. The three aircraft made a successful landfall after the long sea crossing to Java and found the target as briefed. Each aircraft made separate bombing runs but almost all the bombs failed to explode and no damage appeared to have been caused to the target. There was no return fire from the ship. A subsequent enquiry came to the conclusion that faulty detonators fitted to the bombs were the cause of them failing to explode.

During the operation by the No. 99 Squadron aircraft, Lieutenant Valk of No. 321 Squadron was airborne in Canso 'Q' for a total of 12 hours 30 minutes to provide air/sea rescue assistance if it was required.

The experiences of the personnel of other heavy bomber squadron, No. 356 was similar to that of No. 99 Squadron with the aircrews being taken off operations in Burma and given a course on low level supply dropping. The squadron's first Liberator landed on the Cocos Islands at 0700 hours on 22nd July 1945 after a flight of 12 hours from Kankesanturia and the main party arrived with those of No. 99 Squadron on HMT Dilwara.

Unfortunately, within a few days of their arrival, the Commanding Officer, Wing Commander Sparkes, RCAF, developed a respiratory infection and on being admitted to No. 86 IGH, the base hospital, Poliomyelitis (infantile paralysis) was diagnosed. The hospital staff and craftsmen of the Royal Engineers worked frantically to construct an iron lung and a priority signal was sent to Ceylon to have one flown out. This arrived on the first of No. 203 Squadron's newly acquired Sunderland flying boats but was too late to save the life of this Officer and he died on 11th August 1945.

Wing Commander Sparkes was buried on a small island which had been set aside as a cemetery. The funeral was attended by Major General Durrant, OBE, DFC, SAAF who had taken over as Fortress Commander, and Officers and men of the various units stationed on the islands. The bearers were Officers and NCO's of the Royal Canadian Air Force, who comprised a large part of No. 356 Squadron's aircrew. A few weeks after his death it was announced that Wing Commander Sparkes had been awarded the Distinguished Service Order. Squadron Leader Evans, AFC, assumed command of the Squadron.

As the base became fully operational there was a relaxing of security and an operative directive was issued in respect of what publicity could be released. This was to the effect that there was to be no reference to the Cocos Islands being an offensive base nor that there were heavy bombers based there. No reference was to be made identifying the Fortress Commander nor that a Cable Station had been in operation throughout the war without interruption. It could be stated that Royal Air Force units were based there and that the islands were a Staging Post between Ceylon and Australia. Reference could also be made that the Allied Air Commander-in-Chief had made a recent visit. Censorship remained and all mail continued to be censored, with each man being allowed one uncensored letter per month.

On 30th July 1945, Air Vice Marshal G. Harcourt-Smith, Senior Air Staff Officer at Headquarters Air Command South East Asia, issued operational Directive No. 27 to the Fortress Commander which amended the primary role of Royal Air Force Station, Cocos Islands from that of providing staging facilities to that of providing a base for heavy bombers operating against targets in general support of the land campaign in Malaya and the Dutch East Indies (Operations 'Zipper' and 'Mailfist') and also to carry out Special Duties in support of Force 136, a clandestine unit operating behind the Japanese lines in Malaya.

The Directive was set out as follows:

(1) OPERATIONAL COMMITMENT AND CONTROL OF AIR FORCES BASED ON THE COCOS ISLANDS. The Cocos Island air base was built originally as a Staging Post on the Ceylon-Australian air route. A small air and ground garrison was established for local defence. The air force being a single engined fighter squadron and a detachment of long range reconnaissance aircraft. The Cocos Islands provide a convenient advanced base for air operations in general support of our forthcoming Malayan campaign.

(2) COMMAND AND CONTROL. Cocos is at present under the control of a Fortress Commander who is responsible to the AOC No. 222 Group for all RAF forces in the garrison. He is also responsible for the conduct of operations in accordance with instructions issued by the AOC.No. 222

Group. No. 23i Group will move to the Cocos Islands when the command of the Fortress will be transferred to the AOC. No. 231 Group. The AOC No. 231 Group will be directly responsible to HQ Air Command for all forces located on the islands. He will also be responsible for the conduct of operations in accordance with instructions issued by this HQ. He will be responsible to the AOC No. 222 Group for control of LRGR operations in accordance with the Policy Directive issued by No. 222 Group.

(3) FORCES AVAILABLE. No. 136 Spitfire Squadron, No. 321 Liberator Squadron, No. 99 Liberator Squadron, No. 356 Liberator Squadron, a detachment of PRU Mosquitoes of No. 684 Squadron, a detachment of ASR Catalinas. It may later be necessary to base two further heavy bomber squadrons in the islands. Planning and provisioning is to allow for this. Should the additional two heavy bomber squadrons move to the Cocos Islands it will be on or about 15th October 1945, meanwhile these squadrons will continue to operate from Bengal until such time as the move to Cocos. While in Burma they will remain under the command of No. 184 Wing and under the operational control of HQ ACSEA.

(4) INTER THEATRE BOUNDARIES. A common zone of operations between ACSEA and the South West Pacific theatre of operations is defined in this Headquarters Operative Directive No. 26. Operations beyond the bounds of ACSEA boundaries must conform to the procedure and instructions contained therein.

(5) The primary object of RAF Cocos Forces will be heavy bomber attacks against targets in general support of the land campaign in Malaya ('Zipper' and 'Mailfist'). In furtherance of certain deceptive measures prior to the initiation of the land operations. No air operations are to be taken against targets in Malaya southeast of a line

Singapore-Penang, prior to 'D' day. Strikes against shipping and attacks against shipping are however to be undertaken whenever the opportunity arises. In agreement with the South West Pacific theatre there is to be no air mining of Malayan waters at present. The importance of clandestine warfare and the urgent need of intelligence sources to be established in Malaya, call for the extensive SD operations from Cocos. The restriction on bombing in Malaya and the adjacent territories prior to 'D' day, does not preclude strikes against enemy airfields in Java and Sumatra should they offer worthwhile targets. From the foregoing review of operational commitments, the order of priority for tasks are;

(i)   Shipping strikes (against enemy ships in harbour),primary by LRGR aircraft supported by heavy bomber effort when type of target and circumstances justify such diversion.

(ii) For the present, S.D.operations are the primary role of the H.Q. The operations are to be regarded as secondary in importance only to attacks on opportunity targets as defined in para 5(i) above.

(iii) Strikes on airfields should favourable targets present themselves. No. 129 Staging Post will continue to provide normal staging facilities for visiting aircraft and passengers and RAF Brown will provide domestic, administration and other facilities to the units detailed.

On 2nd August Flight Sergeant Green of No. 136 Squadron undershot the runway on his landing approach and hit the taxi track causing his starboard undercarriage to collapse. Fortunately he was uninjured.

On the same day, Flying Officer St. John was detailed to carry out an unarmed reconnaissance in the Sunda Straits area in No. 203 Squadron's 'R'. As he approached the Straits he sighted two enemy aircraft which appeared to be 'Val' Navy dive bombers, one of which commenced to line up for an attack on the Liberator. Both the tail and mid upper gunners opened fire and the 'Val' turned away without pressing home his attack.

On 3rd August Lieutenant Wanroot of No. 321 Squadron carried out an unarmed reconnaissance along the Java side of the Sunda Straits in aircraft 'M'. At 22.59 hours a 90 foot long vessel was seen with a 40.mm gun fitted to the stern. A few round were fired at the Liberator but no hits or damage was caused.

On the 4th August Lieutenant Commander de Bruyn in No. 321's 'Y' and Lieutenant Hufelt in 'V' joined Flight Lieutenant MacDonald in No 203's 'N' and flew to Tjilatjap Harbour on the south coast of Java to carry out an attack on the 3,000 ton vessel that had been the target for No. 99 Squadron's unsuccessful attack a few days earlier.

The three aircraft made a successful landfall after flying over 800 miles at low level and almost immediately located the target. Lieutenant Commander de Bruyn carried out the first attack, dropping eight 250lb GP bombs from 90 feet. Three hits on the ship were claimed and two hits on a nearby floating crane, leaving both on fire. As he pulled away after the attack he saw another 300 foot vessel under construction in the harbour. Anchored in mid stream was a small coaster which he attacked with machine gun fire also some small wooden vessels which were lying alongside the jetty, some oil tanks and a train which was in a railway station. In all he was over the town for 15 minutes but attracted no return fire from any source.

Lieutenant Hofelt carried out his attack on the original target, dropping nine 250lb GP bombs from 100 feet. He claimed one hit on the ship and several on the quayside and warehouses. Flight Lieutenant MacDonald made his attack on the ship from 200 feet and claimed near misses beside the vessel, which was left burning. All three Liberators joined up and returned to base after flights of II hours.

While the three aircraft were carrying out a successful shipping strike, Squadron Leader Fletcher of No. 203 Squadron was also airborne on an unarmed reconnaissance patrol over the Sunda

Straits. During the patrol he saw two coastal vessels being escorted by a submarine chaser which opened ineffective fire on him from a distance of 2 miles. On the return flight one of the aircraft's engines failed and had to be feathered but a safe landing was made on reaching the base.

No. 321 Squadron supplied Canso 'J', piloted by Lieutenant Commander Aerant, to patrol the prescribed route of the Liberators as air/sea rescue back-up. For the crews of the slow flying Canso aircraft the patrols were long and tedious but in Japanese controlled airspace they were required to be ever vigilant. Their presence on patrol and that of the High Speed Launches was a great comfort to the bomber crews who knew that should they be forced to ditch in the ocean, they had a reasonable chance of being rescued.

On the 5th August, Major General J.J. Durrant CB, DFC, SAAF, the AOC of No. 231 Group arrived on the islands to carry out a tour of inspection of the base which he was shortly to take over as Fortress Commander.

On the 6th August 1945, the American Air Force dropped the first atomic bomb on Japan, destroying the city of Hiroshima and in doing so did more to hasten the end of the war with the Japanese than any other operation.

The same day the Dutch Squadron's Lieutenant's Wanroot and Petschi carried out an anti-shipping patrol in 'M' and 'Z' from Balimbing Point to Benkeolen Harbour, Sumatra. During the course of the patrol no shipping was seen but as the two Liberators neared the airfield at Mana, a Japanese aircraft, believed to have been an 'Oscar', was seen to take off and climb towards them. Both of the two Allied aircraft flew into cloud and on emerging found that they had lost the enemy aircraft. Due to this encounter too much time had been lost for them to complete their allotted patrol. Lieutenant Petschi's 'M' had developed a fuel leak making it imperative for him to return to base. Both aircraft landed safely.

At the beginning of August, intelligence reports were received which indicated that the Japanese appeared to be re-enforcing their airfields at Benkeolen, Sumatra. No. 175 Wing immediately made plans for an attack on these airfields and four aircraft from No. 99 Squadron and three from No. 356 Squadron were briefed for the operation. As the ground staff sweated to prepare the aircraft for the operation and the aircrew received their final briefing they were not to know that this was to be No. 356 Squadron's first and last bombing mission of the war against Japan from the Cocos Islands, it was also to the last bombing mission undertaken by the Royal Air Force in World War II.

Shortly before 1300 hours on the 7th August 1945, the seven aircraft, each laden with 3 tons of bombs made up of twelve general purpose bombs fitted with eleven second delayed action fuses, took off at one minute intervals for the 800 mile flight to the airfields of Sumatra. On take off there was 8/10th cumulus cloud over the Cocos Islands with the base being at 1,500 feet and the tops rising to 6,000 feet. The cloud base decreased over the sea but on reaching the target area it had risen to 3,000 feet with good all round visibility.

The Captains of the No. 99 Squadron aircraft taking part in the raid were Flight Lieutenant Archer, Flight Lieutenant Davey, Flying Officer Bonner and Flying Officer Drew.

No. 356 Squadron's records are more detailed, listing the crew members in full. Liberator KN752 'F' carried Flight Lieutenant H.L. Bray, as Captain; Flying Officer E.C. McMillan, RCAF, 2nd pilot; Flying Officer J.L. McBride, RCAF, navigator; Flying Officer L.E. McDonald, RCAF, wireless operator; Flying Officer P.R. Hunting, RCAF, air bomber; Flight Sergeant A.J. McDougall, Flight Engineer; Flight Sergeant R.H. Hammond, RCAF, Front Gunner; Flight Sergeant D.L. Fife, RCAF, Rear Gunner and Flight Sergeant J.A. Price, Upper Gunner.

Aircraft KL654 'R' was Captained by Flight Lieutenant M.C. McNabb; Flying Officer R.R. Halstead, RCAF was 2nd pilot; Flying Officer K.R. Potter, RCAF, navigator; Flying Officer D.P. Bilton, RCAF, wireless operator; Flying Officer H.W. Bradshaw, RCAF, Air Bomber; Flying Officer S. Turner, Flight Engineer; Flight Sergeant F. Grant, Front Gunner; Flight Sergeant J.D. Cunningham, RCAF, Rear Gunner and Flight Sergeant J.P. Richards, Upper Gunner.

Aircraft KH120 'X' had Flying Officer C.F. Schmoyer as Captain; Flying Officer J.C. Huey, RCAF, 2nd pilot; Flight Lieutnant J.P. Campbell, RCAF, Navigator; Flight Sergeant D.W. Urquhart, Wireless Operator; Flying Officer C. Cox, RCAF, Air Bomber; Flying Officer A.E. Hessel, Flight Engineer; Flying Officer K.G. Spencer, RCAF, Front Gunner; Flight Sergeant J.H. Nixon, RCAF, Rear Gunner and Flight Sergeant W.D. Watson RCAF as an additional Wireless Operator. The aircraft also carried Master Sergeant Frederick Friendly, a press photographer of the USAAF.

The crews were mostly experienced flyers who had received their baptism of fire over the jungles of Burma and Malaya but, as with every flight, the elements and the enemy made the outcome an unknown factor.

The seven aircraft flew in loose formation and after an uneventful outward journey made a good landfall on the coast of Sumatra. Identifying the target a number of well camouflaged Japanese aircraft were seen parked along the north eastern side of the main airstrip. A new airstrip nearby appeared to be empty of aircraft.

The arrival of the Liberators appeared to have taken the Japanese defences by surprise but as each aircraft commenced it's bombing run, ignoring the airstrip and concentrating on the parked aircraft, they were met by heavy ground fire from 40mm and 20mm light AA guns.

As Flight Lieutenant Archer in No. 99 Squadron's 'P' flew low over the airstrip at the commencement of his bombing run the aircraft sustained heavy damage and he had to jettison his bombs. The navigator, Warrant Officer Wyatt was wounded and the navigation was taken over by the bomb aimer, Pilot Officer L.J. Carter, who later received the DFC.

As the damaged aircraft flew low over the sea back to the Cocos Islands, it was escorted by Cansos 'J' of No. 321 Squadron, piloted by Lieutenant Commander Aerant who passed numerous bearings to the Liberator, enabling it to arrive over it's base safely. Flight Lieutenant Archer made a good landing on the metal airstrip but as the aircraft reached the end of the runway the nose wheel collapsed, fortunately causing no more injuries.

The first stick of bombs that was dropped on the Benkeolen airstrip fell beside two of the parked aircraft causing considerable damage to both. The following Liberator dropped it's bombs destroying or damaging five or six more of the enemy planes, while a third aircraft's bombs straddled and destroyed a radial engined aircraft.

A fourth Liberator hit and destroyed a further five or six of the enemy aircraft. While the raid was in progress a few enemy fighters, mostly 'Tojos' were seen to scrambled from the main airstrip and some harassed the Liberators for over half an hour. One, a well camouflaged 'Tony', the name given by Allied airmen to a Kawasaki single engined Japanese fighter, attacked Flying Officer Schmoyer's aircraft 'X' causing damage to the tail, elevators and rear turret which was occupied by Flight Sergeant Nixon. It was driven off by fire from Flying Officer Spencer in the front turret.

This was to be No. 356 Squadron's and the Royal Air Force's last bombing operation of the war against Japan. It was ironic that as Flight Lieutenant Bray made his bombing run in 'F' the aircraft was hit by ground gunfire and the navigator, Flying Officer J.L. McBride, RCAF, was killed, becoming one of the last of the 70,253 men killed while flying with the Royal Air Force during World War II.

The aircraft sustained damage and on completing it's bombing run the bomb aimer, Flying Officer P.R. Hunting, RCAF, moved out of his position in the nose and took over the navigation. The Pilot, Flight Lieutenant Bray and Co-Pilot, Flying Officer McMillan, nursed the aircraft back to their base and made a good landing. In September notification was received that Flying Officer Hunting had received an immediate award of the Distinguished Flying Cross.

While the six aircraft were attacking the airfield the seventh, No. 99 Squadron's 'R', carried out an attack on the secondary target, Benkeolen harbour, where they left a 180 foot long wooden ship on fire.

Probably because of this most successful raid in which many Japanese aircraft were put out of action, no air attack was launched against the Cocos Islands.

A few days after the raid a signal was received from the Allied Air Commander-in-Chief, reading,' Please convey my warmest congratulations to the Squadrons on their very successful and gallant attack on Benkeolen (7th August). It's grand to have yet another base from which to hit the Jap. Keep it up, every time a coconut'. Brief details of the raid were also given on a BBC news broadcast from London.

While the attack was being carried out on Sumatra, Squadron Leader Stuart led three other No. 99 Squadron aircraft on the long flight to Malaya where they undertook the Squadron's first S.D. mission from the Cocos Islands, by dropping supplies to guerrilla forces operating behind the Japanese lines at a DZ codenamed 'Funnel 1109'.

The same day Squadron Leader Fletcher in No. 203 Squadron's aircraft 'H' went on a photographic reconnaissance mission to Kebatu Island off the coast of Java. At Thwartway Island he attacked a 60 foot wooden vessel, leaving it burning.

The funeral of Flying Officer McBride, RCAF, took place on the 8th August 1945. The burial party were fellow Royal Canadian Air Force Officers and NCO's of his Squadron led by Squadron Leader L.F. Evans, AFC, the Acting Commanding Officer. He was buried beside Wing Commander Sparkes, RCAF, the Squadron's late Commanding Officer.

On the 9th August, the day that the second atomic bomb was dropped on Japan, four of No. 99 Squadron's Liberators carried out an SD operation to a DZ code named 'Tideway 1800', set deep in the jungles of Central Malaya. During the mission two Japanese 'Vals' approached to within 800 feet of Flight Lieutenant Nichols aircraft but did not attack. 'Val' was the name given to the Japanese Aichi D3A2, a single engine carrier borne dive bomber which had been well to the fore in the attack on Pearl Harbour.

A typical load carried on the supply drops would be 12 canisters containing 3570 lbs for a 'free drop' and 21 canisters containing 3420 lbs which were dropped by parachute.

The aircraft of No. 321 and No. 203 Squadrons continued to carry out anti-shipping patrols, regularly visiting the harbours around the coasts of Java and Sumatra and attacking shipping as the opportunity arose. At 0535 hours on 10th August Lieutenant Commander de Bruyn took off in 'Y' of No. 321 Squadron to carry out an armed reconnaissance of the Sunda Straits. Five hours later at 10.40 hours, a 3,000 ton Japanese merchant ship was sighted in the Straits escorted by a Destroyer or similar patrol vessel. The Liberator lined up on the freighter and made several attacking runs but each time had to break off at 1000 feet range due to the intense and accurate fire from the escorting vessel. However, although many shells were fired the aircraft suffered no damage.

By 1110 hours the aircraft was at the extreme limit of it's patrol area and an attempt was made to bomb the jetty and harbour installations at Morak but the bomb doors failed to open. Eventually the bombs were jettisoned on Rakata Island and they returned to base, landing at 1513 hours.

The same day, four aircraft of No. 99 Squadron carried out successful SD missions over Malaya, all returned safely to their island base.

On 11th August 1945 the first edition of 'Atoll' was published and quickly circulated throughout the islands. This was the islands first newspaper and much guile had been used to acquire the materials and facilities to get it published.

John Behague, a member of No. 99 Squadron's ground staff, was the editor, ably assisted by aircrew and ground staff of the two bomber squadrons. The newspaper filled a gap in the life of the RAF and Army men on the islands, by gleaning from the ether, news of worldwide events, sports news and even news from the world of the theatre. Each edition was eagerly scanned and later when supply dropping to prisoner of war camps commenced, bundles of the newspaper were included.

No. 203 Squadron's Flying Officer Webster and his crew also had a memorable day. They had been briefed to carry out a reconnaissance patrol of the Sunda Straits and as their aircraft was 200 yards into it's take off run with the engines building up to full power three cylinders in the No. 3 engine disintegrated. The two pilots managed to stop the aircraft safely and, being 'press-on types', the crew changed to another aircraft and carried on with their mission.

On reaching their patrol area they saw two convoys, one comprised three medium sized motor vessels and two smaller ships with an armed escort. On turning south they saw a second convoy of a 4,000 ton tanker escorted by two submarine chasers. The aircraft was lined up to carry out a low level attack on the tanker but had to break off as, due to crew error, the bomb doors failed to open.

The two escorts put up an intense barrage but no damage was caused to the Liberator which returned safely to base.

As a result of Flying Officer Webster's report, plans were immediately made for a further attack on the tanker. Two crews from No. 203 Squadron and four from other Squadrons were briefed for this operation. For various reasons the other four aircraft had to be withdrawn, leaving Flying Officer Law to take aircraft 'M' and Flying Officer Tetlock to take 'P'.

The two aircraft took off on separate patrols, the Captains having agreed to rendezvous in the Sunda Straits and make a combined attack on the tanker when it was located. They did not meet as planned as the radio in Flying Officer Tetlock's aircraft became u/s and he abandoned the patrol and returned to base.

Some hours after the two No. 203 Squadron's aircraft had taken off, Lieutenant van Rooy of No. 321 Squadron took off in aircraft 'M' on an armed reconnaissance patrol to Varkensmoek. Shortly after becoming airborne he intercepted a sighting report from Flying Officer Law's aircraft. This signal was also received by the wireless operator in Lieutenant Commander Aerant's Canso 'J' who was flying an air/sea rescue patrol along the route taken by the two No 203 Squadron's aircraft on the shipping strike. Two minutes after the sighting report a further signal was received indicating that an attack was being carried out followed a short time later by a number of SOS signals 'from 'M' reporting that the aircraft was ditching and giving a position off Sebese Island.

The Canso commenced to carry out a search but this was abandoned after an enemy vessel was seen and an unidentified fighter approached the slow flying aircraft from astern. During the following three days, aircraft from No's 321, 356 and 684 Squadrons carried out searches to locate the missing aircraft without success. Aircraft 'M' of No. 203 Squadron was to be the last Liberator to be lost to enemy action in the war against Japan.

It was not until 29th September 1945 that the full story of the missing aircraft and its crew became known.

On that date, Lieutenant Hofelt of No. 321 Squadron landed on the airfield at Palang, Java with a load of supplies. When the crew of the Dutch aircraft visited a nearby prisoner of war camp they found Flight Sergeant Milner, the Flight Engineer of the missing No. 203 Squadrons 'M'. He confirmed that on sighting the tanker they carried out two low level attacks, scoring hits with two bombs. As they turned away they were hit several times by anti aircraft fire from an escort vessel that had been screened from sight behind the target vessel. One wing was set on fire but the pilots were able to ditch the aircraft in shallow water off Sebesi Island. The navigator, Flight Sergeant Watkins was killed by flack in the attack. Flying Officer G.A. Law, the pilot, and Flight Sergeant D.E. Olden, the 2nd pilot, were killed in the crash together with Sergeant G.A. West, a wireless/electrical mechanic. Of the remaining crew members, Warrant Officer G.T. Walters, wireless operator, received a broken arm, Warrant Officer R. Key, a wireless operator was injured by shrapnel, Warrant Officer A. Rosenberg, also a wireless operator, suffered spinal injuries. Over a period of ten days this Officer was beaten by the Japanese in an effort to extract information from him. Pilot Officer B.H.J. Elsee, a member of No. 3. RAF Film Unit, was flying as a passenger and he escaped without injury. Flight Sergeant Milner, the Flight Engineer, only received slight injuries. The additional wireless operators were also air gunners. The day following their capture they were taken to Palembang. It would appear that the ending of the war saved the lives of these men as the Japanese High Command's orders were that captured flyers were to be executed by beheading.

On the 9th, 10th, 12th and 13th August No. 99 and No 356 Squadrons continued to fly SD missions to guerrilla and clandestine forces in Southern Malaya, their final SD operation of the war being a Drop Zone with the code name of 'Funnel'.

The supply dropping missions were regarded by the aircrews as being among the most dangerous of all operations, mostly because the supplies had to be dropped from a low altitude at locations which were invariably surrounded by high ground and subject to very bad weather conditions. Between the 9th and 27th August the two squadrons carried out 57 of these missions over Central and Southern Malaya and No. 356 Squadron lost two aircraft and their crews while doing so.

On 18th August, Flying Officer R.H. McLeod was detailed for a daytime supply dropping operation over Central Malaya. He took off from the Cocos Islands at 0927 hours in Liberator KH218 (K) with Flight Sergeant J. Stewart as second pilot, Flying Officer W.F. Skipworth, Navigator, Flight Sergeant S. Aarons wireless operator, Flying Officer E.A. Penfold Air Bombardier, Flight Sergeant C.J.H. Snewing, Flight Engineer, Flight Sergeant R.H. Lacey, Front Gunner and Flight Sergeant F.W. Gonsalves, Rear Gunner.

On correctly identifying the Dropping Zone they successfully dropped their supplies and commenced the flight back to base, over the mountains of Sumatra and then the long haul over the sea. At 2230 hours a signal was received on the Cocos Islands from 'K' which indicated that it was ditching in the sea and giving a position about 200 miles distance.

An immediate and prolonged search was made by five aircraft of No. 356 Squadron assisted by others from No 321 Squadron and high speed launches No. 2562 and No. 2702 of the Marine Section. Crew members of aircraft 'B' and 'H' of 356 Squadron reported seeing a dark object on the sea and a white light flashed twice nearby. They dropped markers until relieved by a Catalina of No. 321 Squadron, but when daylight came, no trace of the lost aircraft or it's crew could be found.

On 23rd of the month, Flying Officer J.S. Watts took off in Liberator KL 654 'R' at 10.30 hours as one of 5 aircraft detailed to drop supplies at DZ's in Central Malaya. This aircraft, with a different crew, was one of those that bombed the airfield at Benkeolen, Sumatra, earlier in the month. The crew on this occasion were Flying Officer E.D. Mason, the 2nd pilot, Flight Sergeant J. Blakey, Flight Engineer, Flying Officer W.K. Dovey, Navigator, Flight Sergeant A. Turner, Wireless Operator, Flying Officer J.T. Bromfield, Air Bombardier, Flight Sergeant R.A. Towell, Front Gunner and Flight Sergeant W. Ross, Rear Gunner. The aircraft was last seen over the Malayan Peninsula and then disappeared. A search by other aircraft and the high speed launches of the Marine Section failed to find any trace.

On 14th August, Flying Officer C.F. Schmoyer set out on a supply dropping mission in aircraft KH 346 'Y' but had to return after 2½ hours flying with No. 3 engine feathered and low oil pressure on No. 4 engine.

The Fortress Commander, Air Commodore A.W. Hunt, who had been in charge of 'Operation Pharos' since the planning stage and whose drive and energy had helped to develop the islands into a first class Royal Air Force Operational Station and Air Staging Post, left on repatriation. He was replaced by Major General J.J. Durrant, CB, DFC, the Air Officer Commanding No. 321 Group.

Following the Japanese surrender, a Church Parade and Service of thanksgiving was held by the Station Padre, Squadron Leader the Reverend Phillips. The new Fortress Commander read the lesson. The spiritual needs of all ranks had been well catered for by the Clerics of the three main denominations and their assistants since the initial landings.

As part of the V.J. celebrations No. 37/13 HAA Battery of the Royal Artillery fired off 64 rounds of surplus ammunition. They had been among the early arrivals on the islands but fortunately never had to fire a shot in anger.

No. 136 Squadron ceased to fly and their Spitfires were dismantled and crated ready to be evacuated with No. 7136 Echelon.

With the cessation of hostilities the flying operations for the Liberators accelerated, their major role now being supply dropping.

The Catalinas of No. 205 Squadron had carried out the first of the survey flights in 1944 and had continued to make regular flights throughout 'Operation Pharos', carrying mail, freight and personnel. The average time of these flights being over 14 hours from their base at Koggala, Ceylon. The crews had also participated in air/sea rescue flights and had operated a direct service through to Australia.

During June the Squadron commenced to convert to the giant four engined Sunderland flying boats. They received their first machine on the 8th August and by the end of September had eleven. With the larger aircraft they were able to carry many more tons of parachute supply canisters containing medical and Red Cross supplies for delivery by the Cocos based Liberators on 'Operation Mastiff'. They continued to operate these flights until moving to Singapore when it was reoccupied by the Allies.

A Liberator from one of the Cocos squadrons, 1945.

CHAPTER 12

Operations 'Birdcage' and 'Mastiff'

A NEW SERIES OF OPERATIONS commenced on 20th August 1945. Initially involving only No. 99 and No. 356 Squadrons many other squadrons later took part. The first, codenamed 'Birdcage' involved pairs of aircraft flying to towns, prisoner of war and civilian internment camps on Java, Sumatra and Malaya, where they dropped leaflets informing the inhabitants, prisoners, Japanese guards and troops of the Emperor of Japan's agreement to surrender to the terms of the Allied ultimatum unconditionally. The leaflets warned the Japanese troops on how to behave and also advised the prisoners on how to handle unaccustomed quantities of food that they could expect to receive.

These 'Birdcage' operations continued until 29th August and were immediately followed by Operation 'Mastiff'. The new operation involved all the Liberator Squadrons on the Cocos islands and included squadrons operating from Ceylon and the Australian mainland who used the islands to refuel.

The purpose of operation 'Mastiff' was to drop essential medical and food supplies to the inmates of the many prisoner of war and civilian internment camps in those areas.

The following table shows the extent to which the Squadrons based on the Cocos Islands played their part in the closing weeks of the war against Japan and the early days of peace:

NO. 99 SQUADRON

15 tons of bombs dropped in three operations.
57,000 lbs of supplies dropped in 33 operations to Guerrillas.
10,400 lbs of Red X and medical supplies dropped in three
'Mastiff' operations.
34,600 lbs. of leaflets dropped in 'Operation Birdcage'.

NO. 203 SQUADRON

3.25 tons of bombs dropped in seven operations.
2 Air/Sea rescue operations.

NO. 321 SQUADRON

4 tons of bombs dropped in nine operations.
21 Air/Sea rescue sorties.

NO. 356 SQUADRON

9 tons of bombs dropped by three aircraft.
61,690 lbs of supplies dropped in 28 operations to Guerrillas.
8 sorties flown on 'operation Birdcage'.
13,665 lbs of Red X and medical supplies dropped
on 'Operation Mastiff'.

NO. 684 SQUADRON

35 Photographic reconnaissance sorties flown.
281 hours flown on operations.

In addition to the operations carried out by the Squadrons during
the month, No. 129 Staging Post had received 86 aircraft in transit
and had dispatched 82. Some 420 passengers in transit had been
fed and given accommodation, 13,748 lbs. of freight had been
received and 19,904 lbs. dispatched.

On 21st August, the Chaplain-in-Chief, Cannon R.F. Diggle, MC visited the islands and on the 30th of the month the Right Reverend C.D. Hanley, Bishop of Colombo, arrived to dedicate the new church at South Camp to St. Aiden.

The visit of the Bishop was marred by the tragic loss of the aircraft and crew of the No. 232 Squadron C.87 aircraft EW/622 that had brought him and his party to the islands. The C.87 was the transport version of the Liberator bomber. On its arrival it had been refuelled and serviced by the Staging Post personnel ready for it's onward flight to Australia with just the crew on board. The aircraft took of at 2116 hours that evening, shortly after becoming airborne, one of the starboard engines failed. The aircraft hit the sea beyond the barrier reef and exploded, sinking almost immediately in over a 1,000 feet of water. HSL No. 2562 was quickly on the scene but only a very small amount of wreckage was recovered.

It is recorded that 'on reaching 300 feet the starboard engine of Liberator EW 622 failed and the aircraft turned to starboard losing height until it crashed into the sea'.

The Captain of the aircraft was Flying Officer B.E.C. Ford and his crew members were Flying Officer W.A.J. Dearlove, who had previously completed a tour of operations with No. 356 Squadron, Pilot Officer R.G. Sweetman, Flight Lieutenant S.E. Goldsworthy, Sergeant R.J. Derry and Warrant Officer L.W.E. Hilder. They are remembered on a memorial stone in the War Graves Cemetary at Kranji on Singapore Island.

For some reason there did not appear to have been a Court of Inquiry into this tragic accident until some years afterwards. RAF Form 1180 (accident record card) was eventually completed and it was recorded that the omission of an inquiry was to be deplored but may have been because of the rapid movement of personnel at that time and the pending disbandment of the Squadron.

In conjunction with 'Operation Mastiff', the Squadrons had installed empty supply canisters in every mess and canteen on the island, so that everyone could contribute whatever they wished in the way of extra comforts (eg. soap, razor blades, sweets, tinned fruit, cigarettes, tobacco etc). When these containers were full they were included with the official ones and dropped on the prison camps to bring a little extra comfort to the as yet unliberated inmates.

It was not until the end of September that the pitifully frail men, women and children began to flow through the Cocos Islands in increasing numbers on their way to home and freedom following their terrible ordeals in the Japanese prison camps. Among these ex-prisoners was Lieutenant General Spitz, who had been the Governor of Sumatra until the arrival of the Japanese.

Such was the pace of 'Operation Mastiff' that supplies of containers began to dry up and aircraft had to be diverted to fly a shuttle service from Ceylon with additional ones. The Liberators and Sunderland flying boats operating from the Cocos Islands supplied two thirds of all the prison camps in the Far East with Red Cross supplies but the cost in aircraft and aircrews was high.

On 1st September 1945, Flying Officer J.E.H. Steele of No. 99 Squadron was engaged in dropping supplies to the prisoners of war at Sungei Ron prison camp near Palembang on Sumatra. Having made his final low level run to drop his remaining canisters his Liberator, KL.491, was seen to make a steep turn and to the horror of the watching prisoners, the wing tip touched the ground and the aircraft ploughed into the ground in a ball of fire, killing the crew.

Those killed with the aircraft's Captain were Flying Officer J.F. Manktelow, the Second Pilot, Flying Officer A.W. Pearson, Navigator; Flight Sergeant C. Newton, W/op Air; Sergeant J. Martin, Air Gunner; Flight Sergeant J.S. Parkes, W/op Air, Sergeant D.S. Bowden, Air Bombardier and Flight Sergeant Ryalls, Flight Engineer. The crew, who had survived the dangers and rigors of the air war, died on a mission of mercy to their fellow men.

At the time of the crash it was not known how the Japanese troops in the field would react to their Emperor's surrender. A number of Allied prisoners of war in the camp at Palembang were awaiting execution and their fate appeared to depend on whether the Officer Commanding the Japanese troops in Singapore decided to continue fighting. When Flying Officer Steele's

Liberator crashed the reaction of some of the watching Japanese guards was that of delight, which caused a spontaneous reaction among the prisoners, who took over the camp and commandeered food supplies in Palembang.

There were reports that small arms fire had been heard at the time of the crash but this could not be substantiated.

At the time of this operation, Flying Officer Wilson, a permanent member of Flying Officer Steele's crew was detained in No. 86 Indian General Hospital on the Cocos Islands as a result of eating tainted food. They were a very friendly crew and before departing on their mission all the crew members visited him in the hospital. Flying Officer Wilson considered himself very lucky to have missed that last fatal flight and remembers his dead friends with sorrow. It is known that following the crash they were given a funeral with full military honours by the very men to whom they were bringing succour.

During the same operation, aircraft 'K' of No. 99 Squadron had to return to base on three engines. Lieutenant Hofelt of No. 321 Squadron was on air/sea rescue patrol covering the operation and picked up 'K's IFF signals on his ASV set at a range of 90 miles and at a height of 5,500 feet. On making a visual sighting he made R/T contact and escorted the Liberator back to base. Four days later during another operation Lieutenant Hofelt picked up the IFF signals of No. 99 Squadron's 'L' at a range of 60 miles from a height of 1,600 feet. This aircraft was also flying on three engines and was escorted back to base where it landed safely.

A very welcome visitor to the islands was the stage and screen star, Gracie Fields and her husband Monty Banks. They arrived from Australia on a C54 Skymaster of No. 232 Squadron and met up with an ENSA party which had sailed out from Ceylon. The group, which included a number of girls, put on several shows and received a stupendous welcome, although on some occasions Monty Banks received a number of cat calls, presumably because he was Italian – and would have been among our enemies only a few months earlier.

The performances were so popular that the concert party was persuaded to put on additional shows so that most of the troops could see at least one of them. There was even a radio hook-up so that crews who were airborne could benefit from the vocal entertainment. As a result the concert party overstayed their allotted time until a signal, which was prefixed with one of the highest priorities, was received from Lord Louis Mountbatten, Supreme Commander SEAC, who had arrived in Singapore which was to be the concert party's next stop. The signal read, *'What have you done with Our Gracie'*. It caused much amusement, but the concert party had to pack their bags and bit farewell to the islands to which they had become enchanted.

Lieutenant General Wheeler, Deputy Commander-in-Chief, South East Asia Command, passed through the Staging Post en-route to Australia from Singapore where he had witnessed the signing of the terms of surrender by the Japanese Military Authorities.

A not so welcome visitor was the Sultan of Selang. He arrived on the islands in a No. 356 Squadron Liberator from Singapore with three of his staff and an armed military escort to await interrogation for collaborating with the Japanese. He was temporarily imprisoned on Horsburgh Island.

On 31st August 1945 all the members of No. 321 Squadron were given a holiday to celebrate the 65th birthday of Queen Wilhemina of the Netherlands as they eagerly awaited the signal to say that Allied troops had finally re-occupied the islands of the Dutch East Indies.

The squadron did not fly its first 'Mastiff' mission until the 9th September 1945 when Lieutenant Petschi took aircraft 'Y' to the airfield at Kemajoran outside the town of Batavia on the island of Java, where he parachuted 3,160 lbs of supplies on to the airstrip, among which were canisters containing extra luxuries which had been contributed by all ranks of the squadron, also included were 45 personal letters from airmen whose relatives were known to be imprisoned on the island.

All the parachutes were seen to open and land on the airstrip. After the last run, two European and six Japanese men were seen to collect the canisters and load them into trucks. The aircrew were quick to note that the gun emplacements around the airfield were empty. One 'Sally' aircraft was seen to take off and fly North and another was seen in a hangar.

The following day, Lieutenant Wanroot and his crew took aircraft 'M' to the airfields at Padang and Fort de Kock, halfway up the west coast of Sumatra. At Padang they saw that a black flag was flying beside the control tower on which the letters PW were painted in yellow. Beside the airstrip they saw several dummy aircraft and a Japanese 'Sally' aircraft with a green cross on a white circle painted on its fuselage. On this mission 2,980 lbs. of supplies were dropped. During the return flight the crew were very interested to see a 4,000 ton vessel under repair. This was the *Hiyosi Mari*, the ship that they had attacked in Boengoes Bay on 24th July.

While Lieutenant Wanroot and his crew were over Padang, Lieutenant Hofelt took Liberator 'V' to Bankinang prison camp where a number of Dutch and British flags were seen to be flying as he dropped his 4,062 lbs of supplies. The following day Lieutenant Manak in aircraft 'C' returned to the same camp where he dropped a further 3,700 lbs.

The 12th saw Lieutenant's Petschi and Wanroot in 'Y' and 'M' flying in company to Palembang where they dropped 3,865 lbs and 3,550 lbs of supplies respectively on the airfield at Saboking-king. The crews took photographs of the oil installations at Palembang and shipping on the Moesti River.

On 13th September, while Lieutenant Petschi and the crew of 'Y' were dropping 4,340 lbs of supplies at Rantau and Parapat prison camps on Sumatra, Flight Lieutenant Warwick and Flying Officer Jones of No. 684 Squadron were reported missing while engaged on a photographic reconnaissance mission in Mosquito 'X' to prison camps in the Sourabayaja area.

The following day, aircraft from the Squadron and Lieutenant Manak of No. 321 Squadron carried out a search along the sea track that the missing Mosquito was believed to have taken. While the search was in progress, a signal was received that the missing aircraft and crew had made a safe landing on the airfield at Kallang, Singapore.

On 15th September Lieutenant Wanroot and his crew took Liberator 'M' to the airfield at Talanghetotoe, near Palembang, Sumatra, where they dropped 3,970 lbs of supplies. While the drop was in progress the crew saw a number of men waving white flags and the letters 'P.W.' had been marked out beside the airstrip. Among the people seen were an RAF Officer and a number of Europeans, one of whom fired off a green flare. A Dakota aircraft was parked beside the airstrip.

The 15th September was the day when Battle of Britain parades were held at all RAF Stations to commemorate the sacrifice made by those who had fought and died during the long hot summer of 1940. RAF Station Cocos Islands was no exception and a combined Church Service was conducted by the Station Padre, Squadron Leader the Reverend K.C. Phillips and the lesson was read by the Fortress Commander, Major General Durrant.

On the 16th Lieutenant Petsci took aircraft 'X' to the Poebock prison camps on Sumatra where a large number of prisoners were seen waving as the aircraft made its drops. On returning via Eggano Island heavy rain and towering cumulus clouds over Benkoelen forced the aircraft to climb to 14,000 feet in order to cross the Barisan Mountain range to reach the coast.

On the 20th, when Lieutenant Hofelt flew low over the airfield at Kemajoran, he saw five Mitchell light bombers and a Dakota aircraft with Dutch markings parked beside the airstrip. There was no sign of a reception party and he decided to land. Having done so he met an RAF Squadron Leader and a Captain of the Netherlands East Indies Army Air Force who informed him that his own squadron's aircraft were making frequent visits with supplies to that airfield and no other parachute drops were expected. There had obviously been a breakdown in communications between the Allies, all of whom were working at full stretch in their efforts to supply the many prison camps throughout the islands prior to the

A Liberator takes off from the steel airstrip on the Cocos Islands, 1945.

landing of Allied troops. The Liberator was the first to land on the airfield and it was fitting that it was crewed by Dutchmen.

While his colleagues were over Java, Lieutenant Wanroot and the crew of 'M' flew No 321 Squadron's first S.D. mission to Malaya where they dropped 2,846 lbs of essential supplies to resistance troops who were still operating deep in the jungle in the Seramban area. The dropping zone had been given the code name of 'Humour' and on arrival they made two circuits of the area identifying that they were at the correct rendezvous by the 'T' signal of fires which had been lit by the reception party. On their return to the Cocos Islands a congratulatory signal was received from the Force 136 Commander on an excellent drop.

On the 22nd of the month Lieutenant Manak unloaded 3,635 lbs of supplies over the airfield at Fort de Kock, Sumatra and the following day Lieutenant Hofelt and the crew of aircraft 'V' flew to Talangbetoetoe airfield near Palembang. On arriving over the airfield he saw the message 'PW-B24 OK to Land' painted on the runway. He decided to land with his 4,250 lbs of supplies and having done so retrieved the parachutes from the canisters for future use. There was an Army Major in charge of the reception party who informed the pilot that no further supplies were required at Palembang as they were in regular communication with Allied Forces in Singapore and that the majority of prisoners from the camps in that area had already been evacuated. Again there appeared to have been a breakdown in Allied communications or a lack of co-ordination in the distribution of supplies to the many prison camps.

Lieutenant Petschi and the crew of 'T' were engaged on the same operation and when he saw that 'V' had received a good reception he turned and flew to the airfield at Kemajoran, near Batavia with his load of 4,000 lbs of supplies. Included in his load were canisters filled with 3,300 rupees worth of luxuries which had had been obtained from the NAAFI with donations which had been contributed by all ranks of the Dutch squadron.

On the 24th of the month, Lieutenant Commander Aerant, the Commander of the Canso flight, made his first 'Mastiff' flight

TO ALL ALLIED PRISONERS OF WAR

THE JAPANESE FORCES HAVE SURRENDERED UNCONDITIONALLY
AND THE WAR IS OVER

WE will get supplies to you as soon as is humanly possible and will make arrangements to get you out, but, owing to the distances involved, it may be some time before we can achieve this.

YOU will help us and yourselves if you act as follows :—

(1) Stay in your camp until you get further orders from us.

(2) Start preparing nominal rolls of personnel, giving fullest particulars.

(3) List your most urgent necessities.

(4) If you have been starved or underfed for long periods DO NOT eat large quantities of solid food, fruit or vegetables at first. It is dangerous for you to do so. Small quantities at frequent intervals are much safer and will strengthen you far more quickly. For those who are really ill or very weak, fluids such as broth and soup, making use of the water in which rice and other foods have been boiled, are much the best. Gifts of food from the local population should be cooked. We want to get you back home quickly, safe and sound, and we do not want to risk your chances from diarrhoea, dysentry and cholera at this last stage.

(5) Local authorities and/or Allied officers will take charge of your affairs in a very short time. Be guided by their advice.

carrying 2,380 lbs of supplies to Batavia. While still over the sea his Catalina 'J' developed engine trouble and much to his chagrin he was forced to jettison his cargo into the sea. With the lightened aircraft he was able to return safely to base.

Two days later Lieutenant Manak carried 4,500 lbs of supplies in aircraft 'C' to the airfield at Kaliranteng, near the town of Sermarang, Java where he had permission to land. Having made a successful landing the Liberator ran into soft sand and the nose wheel collapsed. No injuries were caused but they had to abandon the aircraft.

A passenger on the aircraft was the new Commanding Officer of the Squadron, Commander C. Schaper, who had assumed command of the parent squadron in Ceylon from Commander W. van Prooyen on 20th September 1945. The Commander was en-route to Batavia where his orders were to make arrangements for the Squadron's move as soon as the political situation permitted.

Commander Schaper continued to his destination in a Japanese aircraft flown by a Japanese pilot while Lieutenant Manak and the crew of 'C' flew back to the Cocos Islands in one of the Squadron's Canso aircraft.

The gleaming white Liberators of the Dutch Squadron's detachment on the Cocos Islands carried out many missions to Java and Sumatra as part of 'Operation Mastiff', some of which entailed them landing on the airfields at the dropping zones to unload their supplies. The crews were amazed to find that even weeks after the end of hostilities, some of the prisoner of war camps and civilian internment camps were still under the complete control of the Japanese, who were now working for the Red Cross and Returned Association of Prisoners of War, India (RAPWI) while awaiting the arrival of Allied troops. The Dutch airmen found the situation most frustrating as many of them had homes and relatives on the various islands. The Squadron was

Preceding pages: front and back of one of the leaflets dropped by the Cocos squadrons on POW camps in Singapore and Indonesia.

under orders to move to Java as soon as practicable but the political situation at the time prevented the move.

There were many rebel forces on the islands who were apposed to returning to Dutch domination, desiring their independence.

In many situations it transpired that the rebels had been actively encouraged by the Japanese. In due course the Squadron did make the move to the islands, so cutting their five-year alliance with the Royal Air Force and reverting to the control of the Royal Netherlands Naval Air Service.

The missions of the Cocos based Liberator squadrons who were engaged on 'Operation Mastiff' were supplemented by the aircraft of No's.12, 15, 23 and 25 Squadrons of the Royal Australian Air Force. These squadrons, flying from Australia, dropped or landed 71,472 lbs of supplies on the Dutch Islands and then flew on to the Cocos Islands to refuel and reload before making the return flight.

The missions of mercy continued and during the month of September 1945 the Cocos based squadrons dropped an enormous amount of supplies on 'Operation Mastiff' and on the SD missions over Malaya.

NO. 99 SQUADRON.

On 23 SD missions – 44,873 lbs dropped.
On 49 'Mastiff' operations – 16,000 lbs dropped.
In addition the squadron flew 210 hours on ferry duties.

NO. 321 SQUADRON

On 1 SD mission – 3,600 lbs dropped.
On 16 'Mastiff' operations – 53,800 lbs dropped.

NO. 356 SQUADRON

On 27 SD missions – 59,000 lbs dropped.
On 49 'Mastiff' operations – 94,965 lbs dropped.

NO. 684 SQUADRON

7 photographic reconnaissance flights undertaken.
3 Courier flights were made.
3 Air/Sea Rescue searches made.

NO. 129 STAGING POST

81 incoming and 81 outgoing aircraft dealt with, together with 29,287 lbs of incoming mail and 17,918 lbs of outgoing mail.

There was such a large number of 'Mastiff' and SD operations carried out during September by the Cocos based squadrons that the supply of canisters began to dry up. As two thirds of all supplies dropped to POW and Civilian Internment Camps in SEAC were being flown from the Cocos Islands, 15 aircraft of No. 203 Squadron were diverted from other duties to fly in extra canisters from their main base at Kankasanturia, Ceylon.

These flights continued until 25th September. Personnel were carried on the outward flight to Ceylon, thereby gradually reducing the men on the base, as many units, particularly Army Units, became surplus to requirements. Even so, by the end of September there were still 94 Army Officers, 4,638 Other Ranks and 186 Army vehicles remaining. The ferrying of personnel by No. 203 Squadron continued until April 1946.

The control tower at RAF Station 'Brown', 1945.

CHAPTER 13

The Run Down

As the Allied land forces began to take over the territory previously occupied by the Japanese and to liberate the wretched inmates of the prison camps, the usefulness of the highly successful 'Operation Mastiff' began to wane and plans were made for the deployment to other bases of the various RAF units on the islands.

The monthly return showing the order of Battle for the RAF units at RAF Station Cocos Islands as at 30th September 1945 were as follows;

STRENGTH	ORDER OF BATTLE
175 Wing	Disbanding.
SHQCocos Islands.)	Remaining on COCOS
No. 129 Staging Post.)	to form one HQ
78.Embarkation Unit	Move to Madras.
737.Forecast Centre	Remaining on Cocos.
No. 99 Squadron.)	Moving when airfields
No. 7099 Echelon.)	are available in the
No. 356 Squadron.)	Singapore area.
No. 7356 Echelon.)	
No. 136 Squadron.)	Probably moving to
No. 7136 Echelon.)	Port Swettenham, Malaya.
No. 203 Squadron Det.	Probably moving to Sarawak.
No. 321 Squadron Det.	Moving to Batavia in December.
No. 684 Squadron Det.	Moving to Saigon.
213 Group Det.	Rejoining G.P.H.Q.
No. 15 MSU (Torpedoes)	Return to Ceylon.

There were still a few more 'Mastiff' operations to be carried out. The last regular scheduled supply drop by aircraft of the Royal Australian Air Force was on 3rd October at Samarang, Java, while en route from the islands to their home base at Truscott, Australia, Aircraft of No. 99 Squadron successfully carried out their last 'Mastiff' operation on the 4th October but the mission ended in tragedy when Liberator 'K', piloted by Flying Officer L.S. Drew, was reported missing. A search by five aircraft over the next three days failed to find any trace of the aircraft or crew.

The final 'Mastiff' operation from the Cocos Islands was carried out by eight aircraft of No. 356 Squadron on the 8th October 1945 when they dropped their canisters over the airfield at Kallang on Singapore Island and the last SD operation was over Central Malaya on 12th October 1945.

News was received of the impending disbandment of No. 356 Squadron and a congratulatory signal was received from Air Marshal Sir Keith Park on the achievements of the Squadron and the superb maintenance record of No. 7356 Echelon during their 22 months of existence.

The Squadron also received a signal from Colin Mackenzie, the Officer Commanding the clandestine Force 136, in which he complimented the aircrews on the accuracy of their supply dropping missions over the jungles of Central and Southern Malaya.

On 13th October, Group Captain Sissons relinquished his Command of No. 129 Staging Post and assumed the role of Fortress Commander. The same day Squadron Leader M.J. Gardener arrived on the islands by Skymaster from Ratmalana, Ceylon, to take over the Command of No. 129 Staging Post. This Officer had completed a tour of operations on Mosquito aircraft in the European theatre of war with No. 157 Squadron. He had volunteered for duties with Transport Command ferrying aircraft to the Far East, which had led to the Command of No. 10 Ferry Unit at Nagpur in the Central Provinces of India. He remained in Command of the Staging Post until the 6th April 1946 when he left to commence the long journey home to the United Kingdom. On the first leg of the journey he shared the cargo hold of a Liberator with the Bishop of Singapore, a recent prisoner of the Japanese.

During the month an advanced party of No. 321 Squadron flew to Sourabaya, Java, to establish an air base for the Royal Netherlands Naval Air Service. Due to the politically motivated unrest and climate prevailing throughout the Dutch East Indies at the time, they were forced to fly on to Batavia until the situation became more stable but on 17th October 1945, the people and various political groups of the Dutch East Indies proclaimed themselves the Independent State of Indonesia although there was much blood shed before the proclamation became a reality.

The auxiliary aircraft carrier HMS *Smiter* arrived off the islands on 14th October and embarked the personnel and crated Spitfires of No. 136 Squadron. The squadron was taken to Malaya where the aircraft were re-assembled and the squadron carried out further flying duties.

With the run down of squadron activities, No. 231 Group and No. 175 Wing were disbanded and the Station Headquarters reverted to working under No. 222 Group who were reformed as Air Headquarters, Ceylon.

The wireless operators of the D/F sections had been very busy ever since the base had become operational. The ending of the war with Japan had caused little let up in their work and during October they gave 66 VHF/DF homing bearings and 143 HF/DF bearings to aircraft in transit with a further 348 bearings given to operational aircraft.

Off duty activities were not all swimming and fishing. Flight Sergeant Evans, a radio engineer in civilian life and a member of a Radar unit on the Cocos Islands, built his own 10 watt radio transmitter and receiver once the war was over. As not all receivers can pick up short wave transmissions, his parents, who lived in Maidenhead, England, enlisted the help of some amateur radio enthusiasts in the Reading area and were soon talking to their son over half a World away.

Eric Moore, a Radar Officer on Home Island, remembers the fun that was had with the short wave radio, picking voices out of the air from thousands of miles away. One Radio Ham lived in Yorkshire in the North of England and could only be contacted during the early morning, which apparently made him late for work.

Another exciting contact was with a member of the crew of an American destroyer stationed off Guam Island in the Pacific Ocean who wanted to forge a link between the Cocos Islands and mainland America. He was using the ship's transmitter of about 500 watts as opposed to the official maximum of 10 watt power that the RAF amateurs were allowed and was blotting out all other calls. His first comments were, "Its awfully swell of you guys to give me this call, I would have given you half of my transmitter for it but unfortunately it belongs to Uncle Sam!

Although many units, mostly Army, had left or were leaving the islands, those remaining were fully occupied in maintaining the RAF Station and Staging Post at a high operational standard of efficiency.

Two months after the ending of the war with Japan the following extracts from the operational logs show the activities of the Squadrons and the Staging Post during October 1945.

NO. 99 SQUADRON

On 24 'Mastiff' missions. 61,265 lbs dropped/landed.
On 2 SD missions. 6,002 lbs dropped.
8 Air/sea rescue searches.
21 Ferry flights.

NO. 356 SQUADRON

On 21 'Mastiff' missions. 58,050 lbs dropped/landed.
On 4 SD missions 7,614 lbs dropped.
32 Ferry Flights.

NO. 129 STAGING POST

55 Aircraft were handled.
260 Passengers passed through.
434 Passengers dispatched.
76 Passengers disembarked.
25,619 lbs of freight received and 5431 lbs dispatched.
16,704 lbs of mail received and 11,390 lbs dispatched.
47 crews were briefed on the Ceylon-Australia routes which
were from Ratmalana and China Bay in Ceylon and through to
Perth and Minneriga, Australia.

On the site that was occupied by the Staging Post a number of
permanent buildings had been erected. These included an
Officers Mess, Sergeants Mess and dining hall, and an Airmen's
dining hall with showers attached. For those men and women
passing through the island base a Transit Mess of four large and
airy 'bashers' complete with showers and ablutions had been
built. In addition there was a Church, Corporals Club, Reading
Room and a large Garrison Theatre. For those in transit, swimming had been arranged on a safe beach on Direction Island and
for a small fee tuition in sailing could be arranged.

At the beginning of November the last Mosquitoes of the
Photographic Reconnaissance Detachment of No. 684 Squadron
flew off to re-join the parent Squadron which had moved to Tan
Son Nhut, in the Saigon area of Vietnam. The base's two resident
Liberator Squadrons, No. 99 and No. 356, completed a further 57
supply dropping missions before departing for Ceylon where
both squadrons were disbanded.

The ground staff of the two squadrons were ferried back to
Ceylon by the aircraft of No. 160 Squadron. This squadron had not
been stationed on the Cocos Islands but had been involved in
transport duties to the islands from the time that the landing strip
had been opened for multi engined aircraft.

In addition to ferrying personnel and the delivery of many
tons of freight, the squadron had also been involved on Special

Duty missions, making photographic reconnaissance flights and dropping agents and supplies into Java, Sumatra and Malaya, many of these missions used the Cocos Islands to re-fuel and as a useful halfway stop.

When the Canso flying boats of No. 321 Squadron left the islands, No. 160 Squadron supplied two Liberators to replace them on air/sea rescue standby duties.

On the last day of July 1945, one of the Squadron's aircraft, BZ 862 'Q', was flown by Flight Lieutenant J.A. Muir on what is believed to have been the longest combat mission to have been flown by a Liberator aircraft in World War II and also the longest made by any Allied land plane. He was airborne for 24 hours 10 minutes and covered a total distance of 3,735 miles.

Squadron Leader Heatherly had successfully flown the first of the Squadron's 'Mastiff' operations but the first flight of a No. 160 Squadron aircraft to the Cocos Islands had ended in disaster. On the 9th June 1945, Pilot Officer Hynes, RAAF. was briefed to fly Liberator BZ 950'H' from the squadron's base at Minneriya, Ceylon, to RAF 'Brown' carrying a number of ground tradesmen and a new Photographic Intelligence Officer who was to set up a badly needed Photographic Interpretation Unit. As the heavily laden aircraft became airborne the No. 1 engine cut out. The pilot was unable to control the aircraft which crashed in dense jungle, caught fire and burned out. All ten passengers and nine crew members perished.

During the time that the Cocos Islands had been developed as a Royal Air Force base casualties to ground personnel had been light but at the beginning of November five men lost their lives while trying to save the lives of two men who, having constructed a raft out of oil drums, were in danger of being swept over the reef into the deep water beyond. The Medical Officer tied a rope around his waist and as part of a human chain waded into the sea but the rope broke and an extension made with pieces of flex was not successful. As more men lost their footing in the deepening water and were swept away, the Commanding Officer of No. 99 Squadron took off in one of the Liberators to try and locate them but without any success. Insufficient remains were found to identify any of the lost men. On the 6th November, the Station Padre held a memorial service for the victims of this unfortunate and unnecessary tragedy near the scene where they had lost their lives. The names of these men were inscribed on a headstone which was later erected to their memory. They were Flight Sergeant Lewis Hopgood, Sergeant Frederick Victor Simmons, Aircraftman Henry Frederick Manfield, Leading Aircraftman Thomas Bloomfield Reakes and Leading Aircraftman Francis Albert Venn.

This was the second tragedy which occurred through men going too close to the highly dangerous reef despite warnings which had been published in Station Routine Orders.

During the last week of November, the islands were the subject of very strong gales, heavy rain and high tides which caused flooding of the airstrip and the surrounding sites, bringing flying to a standstill and causing chaos to the administration offices. With water rising through the porous coral the surface water could not drain away until the tides dropped. It was an odd sight to see vehicles parked all over what had been an active airstrip up to a few hours earlier. Their weight was to keep the pierced steel plating of the strip from being lifted by the water.

Even so, the Staging Post handled 85 aircraft with 39 passengers arriving and 183 passing through. A further 795 passengers were dispatched and 122 made overnight stops.

Among the variety of aircraft arriving and departing, was a Skymaster of KLM, the Dutch airline, whose crew were briefed for the onward flight to Batavia and two special flights of BOAC Lancastrian aircraft enroute to Australia on what was known to the civilian airlines as the 'Kangaroo Route' The later aircraft were conversions of the famous Lancaster bomber and could carry 9 daytime passengers or 6 at night. An increasing number of these aircraft passed through the islands until on the 6th April 1946, following the loss of a BOAC Lancastrian en route from Ceylon to the Cocos Islands, the route from the United Kingdom to Australia was changed to avoid the long sea crossing of the Indian Ocean and they were diverted to fly via Singapore.

As all the operational aircraft had finally left the islands, there were no operational flights during December but two Liberators of No. 1347 Flight arrived to take over air/sea rescue duties. On 31st December Group Captain R.A.B. Stone took over Command of the base as Fortress Commander.

Many distinguished visitors passed through the islands. An Avro York of RAF Transport Command arrived carrying Field Marshal Lord Alan Brooke KCB, GCB. Chief of the Imperial General Staff and Chairman of the Chiefs of Staff Committee and Mr Webb, the New Zealand Prime Minister. The Avro York was another direct descendant of the Lancaster Bomber having been designated as Avro's type 685 as early as 1942, the first prototype flying on the 5th July 1942, only a few months after the first flight of the Lancaster.

The aircraft of No. 160 and 203 Squadrons continued with the airlift of personnel in place of No. 99 and 356 Squadrons and No. 160 Squadron continued with the twice weekly mail flights.

On 20th December 1945, the Home Island community celebrated the 118th anniversary of the landing on the islands of John Clunies Ross, the first 'King of the Cocos Islands' and founder of their community in 1827, by holding a large party.

Many flights were delayed during December due to bad weather but the Staging Post still gave 29 briefings, mostly to aircraft flying to Singapore, the Anderman Islands and Batavia. The Cocos Island's detachment of No. 321 Squadron had rejoined their parent Squadron at their new base at Kemajoran near Batavia in the East Indies. The Squadron put into operation a scheme to evacuate those of their countrymen and women who had been forced to stay in the East Indies and endure the terror, squalor, privation and rigors of the internment camps under Japanese occupation, by flying them to Ceylon with an overnight stop on the Cocos Islands.

In the first month of the new year, Janaury 1946, the Staging Post personnel continued to carry out inspections, engine changes and general servicing of the variety of visiting aircraft. These included Lancasters, Lancastrians, Yorks, Skymasters, Liberators and Dakotas of RAF Squadrons, RAF Transport Command, QANTAS, BOAC, KLM and even the odd Flying Fortress of the USAF. In all 65 aircraft, 437 passengers, 17,854 lbs of mail and 36,034 lbs of freight.

When a visiting aircraft arrived, all ranks on the Staging Post turned out to assist with it's servicing and to deal with the comforts of the passengers and crew. When the ranks were mingled and all the men were without shirts, no badges of rank were shown. This could be a little mystifying, particularly to members of the two Senior Service where the class structure appears to create a greater division between the ranks than in the RAF, especially during and immediately after the war. It can even be unsettling to a Senior Officer in the RAF, as occurred on one occasion when a DC6 landed and a passenger, who even after the long flight from Ceylon, descended the aircraft steps immaculately dressed in a smart pair of grey flannel shorts and blue silk shirt. He identified himself as a very senior RAF Officer from SEAC to one of the servicing crew and asked to speak to the Crew Chief. The Airman called out to one of the nearby men who was wearing just shorts and sandals, "Hey Dinger, (Sgt Bell), someone wants to talk to you". When the Crew Chief arrived, the Officer (an Air Vice Marshal), said, "Would you arrange to take me to your CO?" The Sergeant pointed to a shirtless man who was standing high up on the mainplane of the aircraft busily pouring petrol through a chamois filter and said, "That's the Squadron Leader Sir." To get the job done in the shortest time it was a question of 'All hands to the pumps'.

During the latter months of 1945 the Air Ministry was concerned with the future commitments of the Royal Air Force worldwide and among the many decisions to be taken was that of the future of the Cocos Islands as an Air Force Base and Staging Post. Consideration was given to leaving it on a care and maintenance footing and reserve Staging Post once the Singapore airfields became available.

On 30th January 1946 it was suggested that the islands be abandoned by the Royal Air Force. The remaining 2,300 tons of bombs, 200 tons of packed petrol, the RAF and Army MT vehicles and stores to be disposed of at sea if they could not be economically returned to a mainland. An effective date for the abandonment was given as 1st November 1947 but this was soon altered and the withdrawal dates given as the last week of March and the first week of April 1946 , the final date to be 19th April 1946.

The month of February brought more tropical storms, causing flooding of the airstrip and the cancellation and delay of several flights. Briefings were given to 61 crews and 57 aircraft were received and dispatched. 78 passengers arrived and 166 were sent off with another 134 passing through. Some 13,236 lbs of mail and 26,039 lbs of freight were handled.

Two Liberators of No. 1437 Flight arrived to take over the air/ sea rescue duties of No. 1347 Flight who returned to India. HMT *Llanstephen Castle* anchored in the lagoon, on 16th February bringing relief for some of the personnel who were long overdue for repatriation. She had been due to arrive on 27th December 1945. This ship was a converted Union Castle liner and a veteran of the Artic Convoys. In 1941 she had carried one of the first Hurricane Squadrons to operate in Russia.

Squadron Leader J.H.A. Boynes arrived to take over the command of the RAF Station and to commenced preparations to close the base down as an operational RAF Station. On 23rd March 1946, the base became a hive of activity when it was learned that a Lancastrian aircraft, G-AGLX, of QANTAS, the Australian Airline, had disappeared on a flight from Negombo, Ceylon to Australia. The aircraft had been due to call at the Cocos Islands to refuel but after making one of it's periodic radio calls nothing further was heard.

A massive air search was mounted which was controlled from RAF Cocos Islands. Ten aircraft of No. 1346 flights, No. 160 and 203 Squadrons, together with Catalina flying boats of QANTAS and the Royal Australian Air Force were involved. During the search some 150,000 square nautical miles of the Indian Ocean were covered and 58,000 track miles were flown. A small amount of wreckage was seen but nothing else. No satisfactory explanation has emerged as to the fate of the aircraft.

The personnel of No. 129 Staging Post did a magnificent job in refuelling and servicing the aircraft, briefing the crews and providing messing and accommodation for those engaged in the search.

Following the loss of Lancastrian G-AGLX a W/T message was sent to the Fortress Commander on the Cocos Islands from the senior Captain of QANTAS on behalf of QANTAS Empire Airways while he was en-route to Australia in another Lancastrian, G-AGMD. It read;

> *'On behalf of my Company I desire to thank you and all under your command with particular reference to O/C 129 Staging Post, his Officers and OR's, for splendid assistance accorded throughout the search carried out in your area following the disapperance of Lancastrian G-AGLX'.*

In addition to dealing with the needs of the search aircraft, the Staging Post gave 61 briefings to other aircrew and 57 aircraft were seen in and out. 78 passengers arrived and 166 were dispatched. Most of the latter were commencing the long journey home for demobilisation, while a further 134 passengers passed through the islands. 13,235 lbs of mail and 26,039 lbs of freight were handled.

The three months up until March 1946 saw the beginning of the final evacuation of the Cocos Islands by the Army and the Royal Air Force, with the Marine Section and Radar Units on Direction Island being evacuated on 16th March, leaving the small island to the care of the Cable and Wireless staff.

Between 1st and 8th April 1946, the staff of the Staging Post gave 19 briefings with 19 aircraft arriving and 21 being dispatched. 2,845 lbs of mail and 4,247 lbs of freight were handled and then on the 9th April all the remaining staff of No. 129 Staging Post were absorbed into RAF Station Cocos Islands.

The seven ships that were used in the final stages to remove the many tons of equipment, stores and personnel were, the SS *Ashville*, SS *Empire Seahawk*, SS *Empire Marshall*, SS *Monowai*, SS *Samspelga*, SS *Aronda* and HMT.3502.

The SS *Samspelga* was loaded with the boats of the Marine Section and the SS *Monowai* and HMT 3502 were loaded with MT vehicles and quantities of unused explosives and pyrotechnics. Over 2,300 tons of bombs, 200 tons of packed petrol and many other MT vehicles were loaded on to landing craft and taken out to sea where they were dumped in deep water. Large quantities of other unwanted equipment was bulldozed into the sea, it being considered too costly to transport it back to a mainland.

An Army Officer and a squad of British Other Ranks arrived and with due reverence recovered the bodies of Servicemen who had been buried on the islands. Under an arrangement with the Imperial War Graves Commission the bodies were taken to a war graves cemetery at Singapore where they were re-interred with a simple ceremony by Service Padres, to lie with the thousands of their compatriots who would not be returning to their homeland. On 19th April 1946, the Royal Air Force Ensign was lowered for the last time and the airstrip and buildings were left in good order to the care of Mr D.A. Somerville, the islands' Civil Affairs Officer.

The remaining personnel embarked on the SS *Aronda*, which sailed at 1300 hours the following day, so ending an era in the annals of the Royal Air Force and bringing to a close a chapter in the history of the Cocos/Keeling Islands.

· Part III ·
1947 - 1988

Landing craft prepare to remove men and materials from the Cocos Islands, 1946.

CHAPTER 14

Return to Peace

CONCEIVED WHILE THE DARK CLOUDS of war engulfed Britain and her Allies as they engaged in a bloody struggle against a modern country whose military had reverted to the barbarism of a primitive age, the Royal Air Force Station Cocos Islands and No. 129 Staging Post were built by a few thousand men of the Armed Forces who had been sent several hundred miles across an ocean which was largely dominated by the enemy's Navy with little protection against air or surface attack other than standard issue small arms. Had such an attack occurred they had little chance of surviving and no hope of speedy relief. No doubt these men would have been remembered in history along with the brave men of Wake Island in the Pacific who put up a spirited and successful resistance against an enemy of superior numbers only to be unnecessarily sacrificed by the tardy reaction of the Senior Naval officers of a nearby fleet.

Through sheer physical hard labour, they had built and operated a heavy bomber and reconnaissance base which, through the valour of the aircrews, had commenced to play an active and essential role in the Far Eastern Theatre of War.

Japan had never ratified the 1929 Geneva Prisoner of War Convention and continued to adhere to the precepts of its ancient military code of *bushido*, which regarded anyone taken as a prisoner in conflict to be a contemptible coward bereft of honour, who had forfeited all right to humane consideration.

Every member of aircrew who was engaged in operations over Japanese occupied territory knew that in the event of having to land in such territory no mercy could be expected from his Japanese captors who had been instructed by their Military High Command to execute all captured Allied airmen by beheading.

It is to the credit of all Allied aircrews operating in the Far Eastern theatre of war, that with this knowledge they continued to give of their best in the battle against the many factors which could result in their becoming captives of the Japanese.

When hostilities finally ceased, the aircrews continued with their fight against the elements of nature and mechanical failure to bring relief to the inmates of the various prisoner of war and civilian internment camps throughout the Far East who had been subjected to the barbaric behaviour of their Japanese captors by supplying them with much needed food and medical supplies from the air.

In the course of six weeks, Liberators operating from the Cocos Islands had delivered 107 tons of supplies to clandestine groups operating in Malaya and 137 tons of essential Red Cross supplies to the prison camps of Java and Sumatra. Aircraft of the Royal Australian Air Force had joined in the missions of mercy by delivering a further 31 tons of Red Cross supplies to those islands, using the Cocos Islands to refuel.

After a long absence, Mrs Rose Clunies Ross and her family returned to their home on the islands in 1949 where her eldest son, John Cecil Clunies Ross prepared to take up the mantle and become the fifth 'King of the Cocos Islands'. Born in London in 1928 he had remained in the United Kingdom during the war where he had completed his education by studying estate management and learning the Malayan language. On a return visit to the United Kingdom in 1951 he married a Miss Daphne Parkinson.

In the early post war years the Australian Government offered to take over the sovereignty of the Cocos islands from the United Kingdom. Having costed the repair and maintenance of the existing wartime airstrip, they expressed willingness to invest £500,000 (Aus) plus £50,000 (Aus) per year to reopen the airstrip and make it part of the South African - Australian air link. As the islands were no longer self supporting they also offered to re-settle some of the island population on the island of Borneo.

On receiving the offer, the British Government called a meeting of the Chiefs of Staff for them to consider the strategic importance of the islands to Britain. Following due deliberation the Committee expressed the opinion that, although the development of the airstrip by the Australian Government for the use of civil air companies would be a military advantage, they could not justify on strategic grounds the retention of an unused airstrip on the islands in peacetime.

In 1950, the Australian Government were informed that the United Kingdom would be prepared to agree to the use of the Cocos Islands by Australia in peacetime subject to the following conditions;

'The Cocos Islands would continue to be part of the Colony of Singapore for all purposes, ie. part of the United Kingdom Territories'.

The Governor of Singapore was informed by letter on the 7th December 1950 of the Australian proposal and the British reply.

At the time that these matters were being deliberated upon the population of the islands was 16 Europeans, 10 Chinese, 1,736 Malayans and 1 Indian.

The Australian Government accepted the answer to their proposal and by an agreement signed on 2nd November 1951 they brought a large part of West Island from John Clunies Ross and built a new airstrip alongside the old wartime one.

The new airstrip was opened in September 1952 and was first used during an inaugural flight by an aircraft of QANTAS Empire Airways flying from Sidney, Australia to South Africa.

With the opening of the new airstrip, Trans Australian Airways commenced to fly a weekly air service from Perth, Australia to Christmas Island via the Cocos Islands. This service, together with increasing traffic on the regular Australia-South Africa air link, ensured a steady flow of passengers passing through the islands.

The Australian Department of Agriculture built a Cattle Quarantine Station on the islands where all cattle being imported by air onto the mainland of Australia are impounded for several weeks.

The Australian Department of Aviation resurrected the air/sea rescue facilities on Direction Island and equipped six boats, manned by young Australian crews, who maintained a regular day and night patrol over a 500 mile radius of the islands until 1969.

CHAPTER 15

England – New Zealand Air Race, 1953

WITH THE RETURN TO DAYS of peaceful existence following a devastating World War, there was an increasing movement of people between the four continents on business and pleasure. Public interest in civil aviation was growing and air routes were gradually being pioneered to cover most countries of the world. To increase public awareness of the progress made in aviation since the pre-war era of flying, an air race between London and New Zealand was proposed with the Cocos Islands as one of the Staging Posts.

The race initially attracted a large number of entries and promised to be the air race of the century, but for various reasons the withdrawal of many finally reduced the numbers to a round dozen.

It was proposed that the route for the race would broadly follow the line Heathrow, Rome, Bahrain, Masirah, Colombo, Cocos Islands, Perth and so on to Christchurch, New Zealand. It would depend on the range of the participating aircraft whether they would actually land at any of the places named or have sufficient fuel to overfly.

The entrants who finally assembled at Heathrow Airport on the 8th October 1953 were;

TRANSPORT SECTION

Douglas DC6	Capt. H.A.A. Kooper	KLM/Royal Dutch Airlines.
Handley Page Hastings	Wg/Cdr R.F. Watson	RNZAF
Vickers Viscount	Captain W. Ballie	BEA
Lockheed Hudstar	Mr V. Reavely	Rause Aviation

SPEED SECTION

DH Mosquito 41	Mr A.J.R. Oates	private entry
DH Mosquito 41	Captain J. Woods	private entry
Canberra PR7	Wg/Cdr L.M. Hodges	RAF
Canberra PR3	Sq/Ldr L.G. Press	RAF
Canberra PR3	Flt/Lt R.L.E. Burton	RAF
Canberra Mk. 20	Wg/Cdr D. Cumming	RAAF
Canberra Mk.20	Sq/Ldr. P. Raw	RAAF
Vickers Valiant	Sq/Ldr R.C. Oakley	RAF

On 25th August 1953, a few weeks prior to the commencement of the air race, a small detachment of 75 men of the Royal Air Force and 10 Royal Marines, embarked on the troopship *Empire Clyde* at Liverpool Docks, to commence the long cruise to Singapore, where they would be flown to their ultimate destination, the Cocos Islands, to become the RAF Servicing Team for the Royal Air Force aircraft participating in the air race.

On reaching Colombo, the 10 Marines, Flight Lieutenant Collins the Engineering Officer, and some of the Airmen disembarked and were flown to the islands to prepare a camp site for the rest of the party who continued on to Singapore which they reached on 20th September. Two days later the boat party boarded

Lincolns of No. 97 Squadron, RAF, expecting a smooth 1,000 mile flight to the islands, instead, shortly after climbing to clear the Barison Mountains of Sumatra, the aircraft encountered one of the severe tropical storms that occur in that area and the flight was anything but smooth. However, long past ETA, they made a safe landing on the islands and met their rivals, the Servicing Team for the Royal Australian Air Force, members of the Far East Air Force (FEAF) and some QANTAS staff.

Anchored off shore was the SS *Neleds*, a ship which had brought fuel, equipment and supplies that would be required by the Servicing Teams. The Royal Marines had used their expertise in manning some landing barges to unload the ship's cargo, which included, fuel, tools and eight new Leyland refuelling bowsers. The fuel was contained in 44 gallon drums which were very heavy to manhandle.

The RAF party transferred the fuel to the bowsers and then spent a great deal of time practising the refuelling of the expected Canberras and the Valiant in the fastest possible time. The RAAF men were carrying out similar practices.

The small group were visited by the Air Officer Commanding Singapore, Air Commodore W.M.L. MacDonald, CBE, and a party which included Group Captain T.G. McHaddie, DSO, DFC, AFC, CZMC of Pathfinder fame, who were on their way to see the race entrants arrive at Christchurch, New Zealand.

Disappointing news was received that the Vickers Valiant aircraft, a RAF entrant, had been withdrawn, as it had failed to complete its tropical trials to the satisfaction of the Ministry of Supply. The news was received with glee by the Australians who erected a signboard in the RAF camp during the night, which read, "Be in the winning team. Join the RAAF". As a result of the withdrawal of the Valiant, the FEAF men, who were to service the aircraft, returned to their bases.

The first aircraft to touch down on the islands, was the privately entered DH Mosquito 41flown by Squadron Leader Oates, who was en route to London to compete in the race. Unfortunately, after he left the islands, he ran into bad weather, which caused him to use an excessive amount of fuel. Unable to reach the next airfield on his route, he was forced to ditch in the sea off the South Burma coast. The aircraft was a complete write-off but the pilot and his navigator, Flight Lieutenant D. Swan, were saved.

The race commenced at London's Heathrow Airport on 8th October 1953,when HRH the Duke of Gloucester flagged off the first aircraft. All the participating aircraft took off safely on the long haul across the world. When the competing aircraft started on the long sea crossing of the Indian Ocean, a Royal Australian Air Force Maritime Neptune aircraft took off from the Cocos Islands to patrol the approach route to give air/sea rescue cover should this be needed.

The first of the competitors to arrive was the RAAF Mk 20 Canberra piloted by Wing Commander Cumming. He made a good landing but in an endeavour to save time, braked very hard and the tyre on the portside burst, causing the machine to veer to the left and the nosewheel to become embedded in soft sand. The only spare Canberra wheel which was available was for a P.R.3 and would not fit the Mk.20. It was the end of the race for this crew.

While commiserations were being extended to the crew, the RAF Canberra PR7 flown by Wing Commander Hodges, flew high overhead, its extra fuel tanks allowing it to fly direct from Ceylon to Perth, Australia without refuelling.

Within minutes, Squadron Leader Raw, RAAF, landed in the other Canberra Mk.20 and the Australian ground crew had it refuelled and on it's way in a record 10 minutes.

The first of the RAF's Canberra 3's, flown by Flight Lieutenant Burton and Flight Lieutenant Gannon, was the next aircraft to arrive. The RAF team went into action and commenced to refuel the plane, almost immediately they encountered a slight, but time-consuming hitch when a filler cap on one of the fuel tanks jammed on a crossed thread. Worse was to follow, when a fuel hose burst, spraying fuel over the aircraft and members of the Servicing Team. By the time that the aircraft had been dried out and sent on its way, they had lost 22 minutes.

The second Canberra 3 flown by Flight Lieutenant Furze and Flight Lieutenant Harper, arrived 27 minutes after Burton had left. They had suffered a delay at Shaibah, Iraq and a further delay at Ratmalana, Ceylon, which had put them 90 minutes behind schedule. They were given a very quick turn round of 11 minutes by the Cocos Islands Service Crew but it was insufficient to affect their overall flight time.

It was midnight before the Vickers Viscount of BEA landed with their team leader, Peter Masefield and BBC correspondent Raymond Baxter aboard. The BEA team sent them on their way within 30 minutes.

On reaching Perth, Wing Commander Hodges in the RAF's Canberra 7 was forced to retire from the race with an engine fault and when Squadron Leader Raw reached Woomera in the RAAF's Canberra Mk 20 the already damaged nose wheel collapsed causing further damage to the Pitot Head, which had to be replaced.

The repairs took 83 minutes which lost him his chance of first place.

The first aircraft to arrive at Harewoood International Airport, Christchurch, New Zealand, with a flight time of 23 hours 51 minutes, an average speed of 515 mph, was the RAF Canberra PR3 flown by Flight Lieutenant Burton and Flight Lieutenant Gannon, who claimed the first prize in the speed section, the Harewood Gold Trophy and £10,000 on behalf of the RAF. Squadron Leader Raw, RAAF, claimed second place and Flight Lieutenant Furse and Flight Lieutenant Harper came in third.

The Vickers Viscount was the first aircraft of the transport section to arrive at Christchurch but was pipped into second place by the DC6 of the Dutch KLM Airline on handicap. In all, eight of the contestants had completed the race, the others having to withdraw through minor accidents.

With the news that the last of the contestants had landed safely at Christchurch, the RAF men on the Cocos Islands packed their kit and prepared to leave for Singapore and the long trip back to the United Kingdom. Before they left, the Leyland refuellers were sold to the Royal Australian Air Force and the RAF men could not resist having a dig at their Australian rivals, by leaving a large sign on the camp site with the words, "Royal Air Force, Winners of Air Race sited here, September 7th 1953 to November 10th 1953. TOUGH LUCK AUSSIES".

The winning Canberra PR3 WE139, has been preserved and may now be seen at the Royal Air Force Museum, Hendon.

The winner of the speed section, Monty Burton, retired from the Royal Air Force in 1958. He continued flying and flew Dakotas for a private survey company being thrilled to pilot one of the Dakotas dropping parachutist in the film *A Bridge Too Far*. Following an eventful flying career he died at the age of 80 on 29 April 1999.

CHAPTER 16

A New Beginning

ON THE 5TH APRIL 1954, Her Majesty Queen Elizabeth II became the first reigning Monarch to visit the Cocos Islands when she and HRH Prince Philip stopped there while returning from Australia on a world tour.

The Australian Government continued in their efforts to take over the administration of the islands but it was not until 25th November 1955 that they succeeded. On that date, by an Order in Council signed by Queen Elizabeth II. under the Cocos Islands Act 1955 of the United Kingdom, and the Cocos (Keeling) Islands Act 1955 of the Commonwealth of Australia, the islands were placed under the authority of the Commonwealth of Australia.

As the number of Islanders was far greater than the Clunies Ross Estates could maintain, a controlled migration scheme had been stated between 1948 and 1951 and some 1,600 Islanders had moved from the islands at the expense of the Clunies Ross Estates and the Government of Singapore. Some had gone to Christmas Island and to Singapore, but the majority had elected to be re-settled in North Borneo thus reducing the islands population by about two thirds.

There are now two distinct communities on the islands. The larger comprises the Cocos Malayans on Home Island and the other on West Island comprises the technicians and their families who maintain and operate the airstrip and the Animal Quarantine Station. There is also an Administrator and his staff and those manning the Cable and Wireless Station on Direction Island.

When the islands were placed under the authority of Australia, the day to day administrative costs were borne by the Clunies Ross Estates in respect of the Home Island community with the exception of education and medical and dental services which were subsidised by the Australian Government.

The Australian Administrators found that the Islanders were living in primitive condition by modern standards and were bound absolutely by the terms laid down and enforced by the Clunies Ross Estates with little redress. Of particular concern was the lack of elementary sanitation. A number of health surveys were mounted but the problem persisted until a Government sponsored sewerage scheme was introduced in the mid 1980s.

In 1974, the Australian Government invited a United Nations Mission to visit Home Island with the objective of obtaining first hand information as to the wishes of the Islanders in regard to the implementation of the Declaration of the Granting of Independence to Colonial Countries and Peoples.

The Mission subsequently made recommendations on the political, constitutional, economic, social and educational conditions of the Islanders and the Australian Government sought progressively to implement these recommendations.

The first Australian Administrator of the Territory assumed office in November 1977 and a Cocos Malaya Internal Advisory Council was elected in March 1978. During that year the Australian Government paid John Clunies Ross $(Aus) 6,250,000 for the surrender of his inherited rights of ownership of the islands, with him retaining the family home and grounds on Home Island. In 1986 he declared himself bankrupt.

The Advisory Council was replaced by an elected Local Government Council in July 1979 and a Co-Operative was established to run the islands coconut plantations.

This lasted until the 6th April 1984. On that date the Cocos Malaya Council chose to integrate fully with Australia. As a result, all persons born on the islands on or after the transfer of the islands to Australia on 25th November 1955 are now Australian citizens. Those who were resident on the islands before that date may also take up Australian citizenship by making a declaration to that effect.

The copra industry, which had been the main source of income for the Cocos Island community since the islands were first settle, had been declining for many years and severe losses experienced during 1986/87 caused production to cease in 1987.

The Commonwealth Department of Territories Annual reports recorded the following tables of copra exports from the islands.

Year	Tonnes	Year	Tonnes
1880	500	1948	550
1890	750	1954	550
1893	500	1960	410
1895	800	1965	654
1902	400	1970	182
1908	600	1975	300
1910	000	1980	253
1920	500	1984	160
1935	750	1986	118

In 1988 the native community had been reduced to 686 and after 160 years of trading in copra and its by-products, life for the remaining islanders changed dramatically.

As a likely successor for the income lost by the decline in the copra industry, the tourist market was investigated and a luxury holiday centre, complete with all the facilities usually associated with such enterprises in idyllic tropical surroundings was built.

The Clunies Ross family mansion on Home Island was refurbished for the use of guests and chalets were built on West Island where, fifty years earlier, several thousand Servicemen had slept under the stars and the days and nights were punctuated by the smooth drone of the Merlin engines of the Spitfires and Mosquitos and the harsh roar of the Pratt and Whitney Twin Wasps of the four-engined Liberator bombers as they went about their business, carrying the seeds of death to the enemy or succour to the needy. These particular sounds are now silenced forever as the new breed of Jet powered aircraft pass through the islands carrying those who at one time were either a friend or a foe but are now only differentiated by colour or race.

KINGS OF THE COCOS (KEELING) ISLANDS 1827-1978

JOHN CLUNIES ROSS
Born Shetland Islands August 1786.
Married Elizabeth Dymoke 1820.
Reigned 1827-1854. Died on the Cocos Islands 1854.

JOHN GEORGE CLUNIES ROSS
Born London 1823.
Married Supia Dupong 1841.
Reigned 1854-1871. Died on the Cocos Islands 1871.

GEORGE CLUNIES ROSS
Born on the Cocos Islands 1841.
Married to (1) Inin 1868. (2) Ayesha 1895.
Reigned 1871-1910. Died on the Isle of Wight 1910.

JOHN SYDNEY CLUNIES ROSS
Born on the Cocos Islands 1868.
Married to Rose Nash 1926.
Reigned 1910-1944. Died on the Cocos Islands 1944.

JOHN CECIL CLUNIES ROSS
Born London 1928.
Married Daphne Parkinson 1951.
Reigned 1944-78.

The Cocos Squadrons

TERMINOLOGY RELATING TO ENEMY AIRCRAFT AND SHIPPING

The Allied aircrews occasionally reported sighting Japanese aircraft and referred to them by the Allied code name system of identification. Some are shown as follows, together with which arm of the Air Forces they were; ie Navy (JNAF) or Army (JAAF).

VAL   Aichi D3A2 carrier-borne single-engined dive bomber. JNAF.

ZEKE   Mitsubishi Zero single-engined fighter. JNAF.

TONY   Kawasaki single-engined fighter. JAAF.

BETTY   Mitsubishi G4M Type 1 twin-engined land attack aircraft. JNAF.

SALLY   Mitsubishi K1 21 Type 97 twin-engined heavy bomber. JAAF.

OSCAR   Nakajuma Hayabusa single engined fighter. JAAF.

When the terms of surrender were issued the Japanese were instructed to paint a green cross on a white circle on the fuselage of their aircraft.

A SUGAR DOG was the term given to small shallow draught motorised barges. (S meaning targets and D small merchant ships).

When the idea was first conceived to develop the Cocos Islands as an airfield, it was visualised that it would be established as an Air Staging Post, to provide refuelling and servicing facilities for aircraft on the long flight from Ceylon to Australia. Within a very short time the islands potential as a forward air base to conduct operations against the Japanese, was realised. A number of RAF Squadrons were based on the islands and a considerable number of aircraft from other squadrons were involved in keeping the base supplied with men, equipment and supplies. Most of these squadrons had long histories of giving valiant service to the Royal Air Force and it is fitting that these should be briefly shown in this book. The Squadrons were:

No. 99 Squadron	Liberator VI Heavy Bombers
No. 136 Squadron	Spitfire Mk VIII Fighters
No. 160 Squadron	Liberator VI Heavy Bombers
No. 191 Squadron	Catalina Ib & IVb Flying Boats
No 203 Squadron	Liberator VI Heavy Bombers
No 205 Squadron	Catalina Ib, IVb & Sunderland V Flying Boats
No 232 Squadron	Liberator III, VI, VIII & Skymaster
No 240 Squadron	Catalina I, Ib, II & IV Flying Boats
No 321 Squadron	Liberator VI & Catalina III & V
No 356 Squadron	Liberator VI Heavy Bombers
No 684 Squadron	Mosquito 34 Photographic Reconnaissance

In addition, the following squadrons of the Royal Australian Air Force used the Cocos Islands as a refuelling base, following supply dropping over Java and Sumatra from their own Australian bases.

No 15 Squadron RAAF	Liberator Heavy Bombers
No 23 Squadron RAAF	Liberator Heavy Bombers
No 25 Squadron RAAF	Liberator Heavy Bombers
No 48 Squadron RAAF	Liberator Heavy Bombers
No 87 Squadron RAAF	Liberator Heavy Bombers

NO. 99 (MADRAS PRESIDENCY) SQUADRON

Squadron Motif: A Puma-Salient
Squadron Motto: *Quisque Tenaz* (Each Tenacious)

The squadron aircraft carry an identifying tail mark of a white disc on a black fin. The squadron was first formed at Yatesbury, Wiltshire on 15th August 1917 from a nucleus of No. 13 Training Squadron of the Royal Flying Corps. By the end of that month it had moved a few miles away to Old Sarum, to complete its training before being posted to the Western Front in the spring of 1918, equipped with DH9s.

In June 1918, as part of No. 41 Wing, it joined other squadrons to be known as "The Independent Force". This force was engaged on long distance bombing raids into Germany, and during six months of war service the squadron was to suffered very heavy casualties while dropping 61 tons of bombs in 76 operations.

Following the Armistice, the squadron was retained in Europe and engaged in carrying mail and supplies until in May of 1919 it was posted to India, for duties on the North West Frontier. On 1st April 1920, No. 99 Squadron lost its identity when it was renumbered No. 27 Squadron.

On 1st April 1924, the squadron reformed as No. 99 Squadron at Netheravon, where it was equipped with a succession of new types of aircraft as they became available for the front line squadrons.

No. 99 Squadron became the first squadron to be so equipped in each case, and the type of aircraft ranged from the Vimy, Aldershot, Hyderabad, Hinaida and Heyford.

No. 99 Squadron had many firsts. On 14th November 1934, it was the first squadron to move on to the new airfield at Mildenhall, Suffolk, and on 10th October 1938 was one of the first to be equipped with the new Vickers Wellington heavy bomber.

At the outbreak of war in 1939, the squadron was still based at Mildenhall but was flying from its war station at Newmarket, where it was initially engaged with other squadrons in leaflet raids over Germany and on armed reconnaissance, searching for German Naval units.

On 14th December 1939, it became one of the first squadrons to carry out an offensive attack on the German mainland when it supplied 12 Wellingtons to join a force of 23 Hampdens and 7 Witleys sent to the Heliogan Bight to search for the Cruisers, *Nurnberg* and *Leipzig*. The squadron was the only one to find a target when it saw and attacked a small convoy. The attack was carried out under a cloud base of 800 feet and the squadron's aircraft were severely mauled by the convoys escorts and German fighters. Out of 12 Wellingtons, 5 were shot down, 1 crashed before reaching base and one crashed near the home airfield. At this stage of the war the Air Staff had not learned that unescorted bombers were no match for modern fighters in daylight.

On 19th March 1941, the squadron moved to Waterbeach, again being the first squadron to use a newly built airfield, where it stayed until February 1942, when it was posted to India. By November of that year it was in action against Japanese targets in Malaya and Burma.

During the next two years, its ageing and overworked Wellingtons were in continuous action.

With the forming of SEAC in 1943 all the Allied forces were integrated under the Allied Air Commander-in-Chief, resulting in the formation of Eastern Air Command. This comprised 10th United States Air Force, the Wellingtons of No. 99 and 215 Squadrons and the Liberators of No. 159 Squadron, who between them dropped over 1,100 sea mines.

By March of 1944, No. 99 Squadron had carried out 1,000 wartime bombing raids and during the siege of Imphal had ferried many tons of 250 lb bombs for use by the Hurricane Hurri-bombers, who were operating against Japanese targets along the Imphal to Tiddim road from airstrips on the Imphal Plain.

In September 1944, the squadron moved to a new base at Dhubalia, where the crews converted to Liberator bombers. These heavy bombers, with their very much longer range, were able to penetrate deep into Burma and the Malayan Peninsula on operations, some of which were of 16 hours duration.

The first mission that the squadron flew with the new aircraft was on 26th November 1944,when they bombed the railway station and marshalling yards at Pyininana, in Burma.

On 20th June 1945,the squadron was withdrawn from operations and the crews were put on to an intensive course of low level flying and instructions in supply dropping techniques on the bombing ranges at Salbani, in Northern India.

In July 1945,the squadron moved to the Cocos Islands where, with No. 356 Squadron, they operated as part of 175 Wing until November 1945, when they left the islands for Ceylon where they were disbanded on 15th November 1945.

Two days later, on 17th November1945, the squadron was re-formed at Lynham, Wiltshire and equipped with Avro York aircraft as part of Transport Command. A short period of time was spent at Hunstorf, Germany, where it played its part in the Berlin Airlift before returning to Lynham.

In 1949 the squadron was re-equipped with Hastings aircraft, and used these aircraft in 1956 to drop parachutists during the Suez operations, flying from Lynham to bases in Cyprus. from where they carried out their missions to the Port Said area. It retained the Hastings until June 1959, when it became the first RAF Squadron to be equipped with the new Bristol Brittania aircraft.

On 16th January 1970 the squadron made its final move to Brize Norton where it was disbanded on the 6th January 1976.

During the time that the squadron was operating in South East Asia, its airmen had been awarded, 2 DSOs, 8 DFCs, 5 DFMs, 2 MBEs and 1 BEM.

On 1st April 1943,to commemorate the 25th anniversary of the forming of the Royal Air Force, King George VI instigated the award of a Ceremonial Standard for those squadrons that had been in existence for 25 years. No. 99 Squadron was one of those squadrons and received the award from the King at a ceremony in 1949.

It is unlikely that No. 99 Squadron will ever again be reformed, but it will be remembered for many years to come, as one of the Liberators that was used by the squadron on operations in the Far East, and from the Cocos Islands, is on permanent display at the Royal Air Force Aerospace Museum, Cosford.

The aircraft, a Mark B VIII, had been built as B-24L-20-FO (44-50206) and while it was on the Cocos Islands had been flown by the Squadron C.O and the Fortress Commander. It was put off charge to No. 332 MU at Cawnpore, India on 11th April 1946 and was later refurbished and passed to No. 6 Squadron of the Royal Indian Air Force at Poona, where it remained in service until 31st December 1968. It was then placed in storage at Bangalore.

In 1974,the President of India presented the aircraft to the Royal Air Force Museum and it arrived at Lynham on the 7th July 1974. It was taken to the RAF Station at Colerne where it was dismantled before being taken by road to Cosford. Unfortunately the aircraft will never fly again, as when it was being dismantled, the wings were sawn off.

The aircraft is a worthy tribute to the men and women who built, maintained and flew in wartime conditions, the 19,256 Liberators that were produced during World War 2, nearly 2,500 of which were supplied to the Royal Air Force.

Spitfires of No.136 Squadron line up on the runway, Cocos Islands, 1945.

NO. 136 SQUADRON

Squadron Motif: On the side of the stem of
a tree erect, a green Woodpecker.
Squadron Motto: *Nihil Fortius* (Nothing is Stronger)

Known throughout the Royal Air Force as the 'Woodpecker Squadron' it was formed at Kirton-in-Lindsey, Lincolnshire, on 1st April 1917 but never saw action, being disbanded on the 4th July 1918, its personnel being dispersed to reinforce other operational squadrons.

It was reformed at Kirton-on-Lindsey on 20th August 1941 and equipped with Hawker Hurricane fighters, its main duties being east coast shipping patrols, until in December 1941 it was posted to the Middle East. While en-route to this theatre of operations, Japan entered the war and the squadron was diverted to the Far East, where it was soon in operation on the Burma front and in the defence of Rangoon. On being evacuated further west, it was soon engaged in the defence of Calcutta, operating successfully from Red Road (Dum Dum). Throughout 1942 the squadron had many moves and operated from various airstrips until, in December 1942, while stationed at Chittagong, it became one of the squadrons engaged in escorting aircraft supplying the XIV Army.

In July 1943, the squadron was withdrawn from operations to Baigachi, India, where it was re-equipped with Spitfire VCs. After a period of working up it returned to the Arakan front in October where it was soon engaged in very hard fighting. On New Years Day, 1944, the pilots of the squadron destroyed or damaged an entire force of 30 Japanese aircraft.

In March 1944, a move was made to Manipure, where it flew cover to General Wingate's Chindit force. During this period, the Japanese made strong counter attacks and the air and ground crews had of necessity to dig in on the airstrip and to live in underground pits at the aircraft dispersals. They were also obliged to carry out foot patrols at night in some force, in anticipation of

Japanese troops infiltrating onto the airstrip. During the day the pilots had to fly standing patrols over Imphal and escort supply-dropping Dakotas.

In May 1944 the squadron was withdrawn to Chittagong and in July was sent to Ratmalana, Ceylon, where it became non-operational.

In April 1945, equipped with Spitfire VIIIs, the squadron was posted to the Cocos Islands as part of operation "Pharos" to provide a fighter defence from the newly prepared airstrip and where it remained until the end of the war with Japan.

After VJ Day the squadron was stood down from flying duties until on the 4th October 1945 it embarked on HMS *Smiter* to be taken to Malaya. Based at Kuala Lumpur, it was used for anti communist demonstration flights until in May 1946 it was moved to Bombay, India, and re-numbered No. 152 Squadron.

The pilots of the squadron were awarded 4 DFCs, 2 DFMs and were credited with the destruction or damaging of 250 enemy aircraft, including 100 confirmed 'kills', many of which were during the Arakan battles.

NO. 160 SQUADRON

Squadron Motif: A Singhalese Lion Rampant holding a
Singhalese Sword.
Squadron Motto: *Api Soya Paragasamu* (We Seek and Strike)

The squadron was formed on 1st June 1918, but like many other new squadrons at that time was disbanded within a few weeks without seeing any action.

It was reformed at Thurleigh, Bedfordshire on 16th January 1942 as a Liberator long range heavy bomber squadron for eventual transfer to the Far East. While the ground staff were at sea, the aircrew completed their training and were moved to Nutts Corner, Northern Ireland, where they carried out anti-submarine patrols for a few weeks before commencing the long flight to the Far East.

While the squadron's aircraft were passing through the Middle East Command, Air Chief Marshal Sir Arthur Tedder, the Air Officer Commander-in-Chief, detained them to cover convoys to Malta and to carry out bombing raids on Libya and Crete, its personnel being absorbed by No. 159 Squadron, from which No. 178 Squadron was formed.

With the deteriorating situation in the Far East and the squadron's ground staff already in India, matters could not be allowed to remain as they were and eventually the squadron's Liberators began to arrive in India, from where they were sent to Ratmalana, Ceylon, to be reformed on 15th January 1943.

Under the control of No. 222 Group and later AHQ Ceylon, the squadron carried out long range anti submarine patrols, photographic reconnaissance and mine laying patrols and in 61 operations laid 800 mines.

In May 1945 it commenced training for low level SD operations at Minneriya, where Wing Commander McKenzie was appointed Commanding Officer.

On 31st July Flight Lieutenant Jack Muir dropped two British Agents behind Japanese lines in Southern Malaya. In doing so he was airborne for 24 hours 10 minutes, flying a total of 3,735 miles.

Aircraft of the Squadron made many flights to the Cocos Islands, carrying personnel, freight and mail from Ceylon. When hostilities ceased they took part in operation "Mastiff", dropping supplies over Java.

In October 1945, the squadron moved its base to Kankesanturia, in Northern Ceylon, and in November it commenced to fly out the ground staff of No. 99 and No. 356 Squadrons from the Cocos Islands, carrying ten passengers on each flight.

Three of the squadron's aircraft made regular flights from the Cocos Islands, carrying arms and ammunition to Batavia, until April 1946 when the route was changed to Singapore. The last of these flights was on 16th June 1946, after which the squadron returned to the United Kingdom and converted to Lancasters.

Based at Leuchars, Scotland, the squadron was employed on general reconnaissance and air/sea rescue duties, until on 30th September 1946, it was disbanded and re-numbered No. 120 Squadron.

NO. 191 SQUADRON

Squadron Motif: A Dolphin.
Squadron Motto: *Vidi Vici* (I Saw, I Conquered).

The squadron was first formed at Marham on the 6th November 1917, as a night training unit. It later moved to Upwood where it continued to be engaged on the training of pilots for night flying, until it was disbanded on 1st September 1919.

On 17th May 1943, the squadron was reformed at Koranga Creek, near Karachi, India, where it was equipped with Catalina Ib flying boats and engaged on general reconnaissance duties, carrying out patrols over vast stretches of the Indian Ocean, Arabian Sea and into the Persian Gulf with detachments operating from several flying boat stations.

The parent squadron moved to Redhills Lake and then to Madras in November 1944. In April 1945 it moved to Koggala, Ceylon where it concentrated on flying anti submarine patrols off the coast of India.

From Koggala the squadron's aircraft commenced regular flights to the Cocos Islands, the first landing on the lagoon being made by Flight Lieutenant E.J. Didcock, flying Catalina JX374 'Z' with a load of mail, freight and personnel, and on 22nd May Cansos 191 'S' piloted by Flight Lieutenant Kenny flew Air Vice Marshal Cole and Group Captain Edwards to the islands and became the first visiting aircraft to land on the new airstrip.

As the Japanese influence in the Far East waned and their naval units withdrew from the Indian Ocean, there was insufficient activity to keep the squadron active and it was disbanded on 15th June 1945.

NO. 203 SQUADRON

Squadron Motif: A Winged Seahorse
Squadron Motto: *Occidens Oriensque* (West and East)

The squadron was formed at Treizennes in Northern France on 1st April 1918 from No. 3 Squadron of the Royal Naval Air Service when the RNAS was absorbed into the newly formed Royal Air Force.

The squadron was equipped with Camels and mainly engaged on fighter ground attack duties until the end of the war. In March 1919 it was reduced to a cadre but was never expanded. On returning to the United Kingdom it was disbanded on 21st January 1920.

On 1st March 1920 it was re-formed as a fleet fighter squadron at Leuchars, Scotland and equipped with Nightjars and Camels. During the later part of 1922 as part of HMS *Argus* it was sent to Turkey and on returning to the United Kingdom it was re-designated No. 402 Flight on 1st April 1923.

On 1st Janaury 1929 No. 482 Coastal Reconnaissance Flight was re-designated as No. 203 Squadron at Mount Batten, where it was equipped with Southampton flying boats. In February of that year the squadron moved overseas to Iraq, where it carried out patrols over the Persian Gulf. In February 1931 the Southamptons were replaced by Rangoons and in 1935 they were replaced by Singapores and the squadron moved to Aden as a result of the Abyssinian crisis. Returning to Iraq in 1936 it remained there until the outbreak of World War 2 and during 1940 converted to Blenheims. When Italy entered the war, the squadron carried out reconnaissance patrols over the Red Sea until in April 1941 it was moved to Egypt and Palestine where it took part in the Syrian campaign.

During 1942 it carried out reconnaissance patrols over the Mediterranean and during February received some Marylands and Hudsons. By the end of the year it had been fully converted to Baltimores.

It retained these until November 1943 when the squadron moved to Santa Cruz, India where it converted to Wellingtons and carried out coastal patrol duties until October 1944 when it was moved to Madura, where it converted to Liberators. On 19th February 1945 the squadron was moved to Kankesanturia, Ceylon where it was engaged on anti-shipping patrols and transport duties.

On 1st June 1945 one of its aircraft flew from Ceylon to Australia, making the first night landing on the new airstrip on the Cocos Islands and on 16th July. A detachment of Liberators from the squadron was sent to the islands to carry out anti-shipping patrols with No. 321 (Dutch) Squadron over Sumatra and Java. This was supplemented by a second detachment in August.

As well as carrying out anti shipping patrols, aircraft from the parent squadron in Ceylon were engaged in regular transport flights to the islands and also took part in several air/sea rescue searches for missing aircraft. The two detachments returned to Ceylon on 10th August 1945 but for the remainder of the year and throughout the early part of 1946 the squadron continued to provide aircraft for the Ceylon to Australia route, calling at the Cocos Islands to refuel.

In May 1947 the squadron returned to the United Kingdom and converted to Lancasters, operating from bases at Leuchars, St. Eval, St. Mawgan and Topcliff. During 1953 it received Neptunes, which remained in service with the squadron until on 1st September 1956, it was disbanded.

On 1st November 1958, No. 240 Squadron, which had been operating Shackletons from Ballykelly on maritime patrols, was renumbered No. 203 Squadron, and in 1969 moved to Malta.

In 1971,the Squadron converted to Nimrods and with the political situation in Malta becoming difficult, it moved to the NATO base at Signonella, Sicily in January 1972. The squadron was finally disbanded on 31st December 1977.

NO. 205 SQUADRON

Squadron Motif: A Kris and a Trident in Saltire.
Squadron Motto: *Pertiama-di-Malaya* (First in Malaya)

The squadron was formed on 1st April 1918 from No. 5 Squadron, Royal Naval Air Service at Bois de Roche in Northern France. Equipped with DH9s, it was engaged on bombing missions from a number of bases in France during the last few months of the war. Returning to the United Kingdom in March 1919 it was disbanded on 22nd January 1920.

On 15th April 1929 it was reformed at Leuchars, Scotland as a Fighter Reconnaissance Squadron with 29 Group, using Panthers in co-operation with the Royal Navy on carrier operations.

On 1st April 1923 the squadron became No. 441 Flight. On the 8th January 1929, it flew out to Seletar, Malaya where it joined the Far East Flight who were then designated No. 205 Squadron and equipped with Southampton flying boats.

It was the first flying boat squadron to be based in the Far East and was used extensively to carry out survey flights, changing the Southamptons for Singapores and carrying out patrols of the approaches to Singapore, the Nichobar Islands and the Indian Ocean.

In April 1941 the squadron received its first Catalina flying boats and when Japan entered the war the squadron was fully equipped with these aircraft which it used to locate Japanese naval forces. During December 1941, the squadron moved to Batavia, Java, losing several aircraft to Japanese raids. They were forced to retire to the Australian mainland and on 31st March 1942 were disbanded.

On 23rd July 1942 the squadron was reformed at Koggala, Ceylon from detachments of Nos 202 and 240 Squadrons, being equipped with eight Catalinas to carry out anti submarine patrols and air/sea rescue duties.

From Koggala the squadron flew regular missions to the Cocos Islands, carrying freight, mail and personnel as well as operating a service through to Australia. During June 1945 the squadron commenced to receive the big Sunderland flying boats which increased the payload considerably.

When hostilities ceased the squadron moved back to Seletar, Malaya and in 1950 its Sunderlands were moved to Japan for patrols off the Korean coast. On 1st March 1958 the squadron was back at Singapore where it converted to Shackletons and became the RAF's main maritime reconnaissance force in the Far East.

The squadron was finally disbanded on 31st October 1971.

It was a Catalina from this squadron that made the first non stop flight from Ceylon to Australia in 1943 in a flying time of 24 hours 30 minutes.

NO. 232 SQUADRON

Squadron Motif: A Dragon ship under sail, oars in action.
Squadron Motto. Strike.

The squadron was formed on 20th August 1918 from flights of Nos 333, 334 and 335 at Felixtowe, where it was equipped with F2As and F3s. It flew anti-submarine and reconnaissance patrols until the war finished, after which it did little flying until being disbanded on the 5th January 1919.

On 17th July 1940 'B' Flight from No. 3 Squadron was designated No 232 Squadron at Sumburgh and it commenced to carry out defensive duties with Hawker Hurricanes from bases at Castletown, Skitten, Drem, Elgin and Montrose until, during April 1941, the squadron became non-operational. The pilots were engaged in ferry duties and the ground staff embarked on a troopship at Gourock for duties overseas on 10th May. This posting was cancelled and the aircrew and ground Echelon were re-united at Abbotsinch, becoming operational again and carrying out fighter patrols down the eastern side of the country.

The whole squadron was finally posted to the Middle East in November 1941, but on reaching South Africa was diverted to Singapore, where the ground Echelon disembarked on 13th January 1942. The pilots and their aircraft embarked on HMS *Indomitable* and were flown off from a point 50 miles off Christmas Island on 27th January to land at Batavia, Java.

Air and ground crews finally met up on 2nd February at Palembang, Sumatra but the Japanese advanced so quickly that they had to evacuate to Java where its Hurricanes were merged with those of No. 242 Squadron and the ground Echelon was evacuated to Ceylon and dispersed among other squadrons.

On 10th April 1942 the squadron was reformed in the United Kingdom at Atcham and were equipped with Spitfires, becoming operational on 30th May 1942 and operating from a number of bases in England, Scotland and Wales until posted to the Middle East in November 1942.

The squadron played its part in the latter end of the North African campaign and then moved to Malta in June 1943 to cover the Sicily landings. Following the successful capture of Sicily the squadron's Spitfires gave support to the landings in southern France, before moving to Naples where it was disbanded on 31st October 1944.

On 15th November 1944 the squadron was reformed at Stoney Cross, Hampshire as a transport squadron and equipped with Wellingtons. Within two months the Wellingtons had been replaced by Liberators and the squadron was posted to India, leaving on 14th February 1945.

The squadron was stationed at Palem, India and the Liberators were supplemented by Skymasters and later Lancastrians for use on the Ceylon to Australia route.

Two of the squadron's Liberators made the first night landings on the Cocos Islands and continued to make regular ferry trips, carrying freight, mail and personnel until the RAF base closed down.

From 30th May 1946, the squadron operated from Poona, India until being disbanded on 15th August 1946.

NO. 240 SQUADRON

Motif: In front of a hart, a winged helmet.
Motto: *Sjo-Vordur Lopt-Vordur*
(Guardian of the sea, guardian of the sky)

The squadron was formed at Calshot in August 1918 from Nos 345, 346, 410 and 411 Flights, operating flying boats and seaplanes on anti-submarine patrols over the English Channel until it was disbanded on 15th May 1919.

Reformed at Calshot on 30th March 1937 from 'C' Flight of the Seaplane Training Squadron, it was retained on flying boat training duties with Scapas and in November 1938 it received Singapore flying boats, becoming operational in January 1939 but reverted to training duties with Londons in June. By July it had again taken on an operational role.

On 12th August 1939 it moved to its war station at Invergordon and commenced patrols over the North Sea, flying from Invergordon and Sullom Voe. On 27th May 1940, the squadron moved to Pembroke Dock and was equipped with Stranraers, patrolling the Western Approaches.

The squadron moved to Lough Erne, Northern Ireland and converted to Catalinas in March 1941. While still receiving instructions from American 2nd Pilots, one of the squadron's aircraft assisted one of No. 210 Squadron's aircraft in shadowing the German ship *Bismark* on 26th May 1941 before she was sunk by ships and aircraft of the Royal Navy and Fleet Air Arm.

On 29th March 1942 the Service Echelon began the long journey to India and the aircraft were flown out in June to be stationed at Red Hills Lake. By the 4th July the squadron was flying operations over the Indian Ocean and the Bay of Bengal. In December 1944, the squadron commenced to fly Agents and supplies to the Dutch East Indies and, while operation 'Pharos' was still at the planning stage, to fly technicians of the three services to the Cocos Islands to carry out preliminary surveys.

The flights to the Cocos Islands continued throughout the operation and four of the squadron's Catalinas were detailed to make regular flights with freight, mail and personnel.

On 1st July 1945, No. 240 Squadron was disbanded and the same day, No. 212 Squadron was also disbanded but immediately renumbered No. 240 Squadron. It continued to operate from Red Hills Lake and make flights to the Cocos Islands and in August began to be re-equipped with Sunderlands. During November the Sunderlands were used to fly No. 684 Squadron's ground Echelon from the Cocos Islands to their new base at Seletar, Malaya.

On 10th January 1946 the squadron moved to Koggala, Ceylon and on 31st March that year was disbanded.

On 1st May 1952, the squadron was reformed at St. Eval, Cornwall as a maritime reconnaissance squadron, equipped with Shackletons. In June it moved to Adergrove, Northern Ireland where, on 1st November 1958, it was re-numbered No. 203 Squadron.

On 1st August 1959, it was re-formed as a Thor Strategic Missile Squadron at Beighton until on the 8th January 1963 it was finally disbanded.

NO. 321 (DUTCH) SQUADRON

Motif: A flying Bird of Paradise, above it the Lion of Ceylon, in it's right foreclaw a sword, all in gold with a tail of gold and silver and all within a sinopal surmounted by a crown.

Motto: *Nulli Secondus* (Second to None).

The squadron was formed on 1st June 1940 at Pembroke Dock, together with No. 320 Squadron, from personnel of the Royal Netherlands Naval Air Service.

On 24th June it transferred to RAF Station, Carew, near Cheriton where it commenced training on the Avro Ansons of No. 217 Squadron. On completing its training on 28th July 1940 the squadron immediately began flying convoy escort duties over the Irish Sea until on 18th January 1941 it merged with No. 320 Squadron.

Following the invasion of the Dutch East Indies by the Japanese, a number of Catalinas of the Royal Netherlands Naval Air Service arrived in Ceylon and on 15th August 1942, these were designated as No. 321 Squadron, with its main base at China Bay, Ceylon. Detachments of the squadron operated from Africa and those patrolled the entrance to the Red Sea from Socotra, others covered the entrance to the Persian Gulf from Masirah.

During December 1944, the main part of the squadron converted to Liberator Mk.VI's and on 2nd July 1945, a detachment of six Liberators was sent to the Cocos Islands for Long Range General

Reconnaissance duties (LRGR), together with two of the squadron's Canso (amphibious Catalinas) for use on air/sea rescue patrols.

The Cocos Island detachment carried out many long range sorties, including several shipping strikes off Java and Sumatra. With the end of hostilities the aircraft took part in operation 'Mastiff' – the dropping of supplies to prisoner of war and civilian internment camps on those islands – eventually ferrying many of those men, women and children to freedom.

In October 1945 the squadron and its several detachments were under orders to move to Java, but due to the political unrest in the East Indies the move was delayed several times and it was not until the end of the year that they finally moved to Batavia, where the squadron reverted to the control of the Royal Netherlands Naval Air Service.

It was not until 27th April 1959 that the Netherlands Minister of Defence granted the squadron its motif and motto and it was not until 29th November 1964 that these were finally bestowed.

On 1st June 1990, No. 320 and No. 321 of the Royal Netherlands Naval Air Service celebrated their Golden Jubilee with an open day and air display at Valkenburgh, Holland, attended by Prince Bernard of the Netherlands. Both are part of the Netherlands contribution to NATO, flying a variety of aircraft, all of a marine nature.

NO. 356 SQUADRON

Motif: A demi-tiger erased (their aircrafts' tail fins displayed a St Andrews Cross)

Motto: *We bring freedom and assistance*

The squadron was formed at Salbani, India as a heavy bomber squadron and equipped with Liberator Mk B-VIs as part of No. 231 Group. On completing its training on Liberators, the squadron commenced to fly meteorological sorties but it was not until 27th July 1944 that it carried out is first bombing raid. On this date, seven aircraft were briefed to attack Yeo. One aircraft released its bombs prematurely but the other six did not bomb because of cloud. All seven aircraft flew on to Kongyi and bombed enemy supply dumps.

From then on the squadron carried out raids on a wide variety of targets behind the Japanese lines, hitting supply dumps, railway marshalling yards, lines of communication and shipping. It also took part in the saturation bombing of Ramree Island prior to its being recaptured.

Taken off operations in June 1945, its aircrew were given training in low flying and instructed in the technique of supply dropping. On completing the instruction, the squadron was moved to the Cocos Islands to join No. 99 Squadron as part of No. 175 Wing.

The squadron's only bombing operation from the Cocos islands was on 3rd August 1945 when three of its aircraft joined four of No. 99 Squadron's to carry out a successful attack on Japanese airfields at Benkulen, Batavia.

Ten days later on 13th August 1945 the squadron carried out its last operational sortie of the war against Japan when four Liberators were engaged in supply dropping to clandestine forces in Central Malaya.

With the cessation of hostilities the squadron took part in operation 'Birdcage' – the dropping of leaflets over the towns and camps of Java and Sumatra. This was immediately followed by operation 'Mastiff' – the dropping of medical and essential supplies to prison camps in the same areas. These operations continued until October 1945.

In November the squadron flew to Ceylon, where it was disbanded on 15th November 1945.

During the short time that the squadron was in existence it dropped 2,540 tons of bombs and mines and over 388 tons of supplies, together with 122 tons of leaflets.

The aircrew were awarded 1 DSO, 6 DFCs and 12 DFMs. It also received congratulations from the Commander of Force 136 for the accuracy of its SD operations over Malaya and also from the Allied Commander-in-Chief, SEAC for the spontaneous efforts by ground and aircrew in collecting extra comforts etc, which were dropped with the official supplies to POW camps. The AOC, Sir Keith Park added his congratulations for the squadrons achievements.

Men of No.684 Squadron with one of their Mosquito reconnaissance aircraft.

NO. 684 SQUADRON

Motif: A mask
Motto: *Invisus Videns* (Seeing though unseen).

The squadron was formed at Dum Dum on 29th September 1943 from a flight of No. 681 Squadron as a photographic reconnaissance unit and equipped with long range Mosquitos and some B.25 Mitchells.

Made operational on 1st November 1943, the aircraft, fitted with F24 cameras, commenced to carry out missions over Burma, Malaya and Siam.

On the 9th December 1943 the squadron was moved to Comilla but returned to Dum Dum on 31st January 1945. In May of that year it moved to Alipore near Calcutta and in September a detachment was based in Ceylon. In June 1945 a detachment of seven Mk 34 Mosquitos was based on the Cocos Islands, where an urgent and extensive programme of photographic reconnaissance to Malaya, Java and Sumatra was arranged preparatory to the recapturing of these enemy-occupied territories.

This detachment made its first sortie from the islands on 2nd July 1945 and carried out 38 similar sorties by the end of the war. On 31st August 1945, Flight Lieutenant C. Andrews and his navigator, Warrant officer Painter, made history when, through a defective engine, they became the first Allied aircraft to land on the Japanese occupied Singapore Island.

The longest flight made by an aircraft of the squadron was on 20th August 1945,when Flight Lieutenant J.R. Manners and Warrant Officer F.A. Burley carried out a photographic mission from the Cocos Islands to Penang Island off the north coast of Malaya – a distance of 1,240 miles. This involved a round trip of 2,600 miles which was completed in 9 hours 5 minutes.

The detachment left the islands in October 1945 to rejoin their parent Squadron which had moved to Tan Son Nhut in the Saigon area of Vietnam.

In August 1945 the Squadron received some Beaufighters and in December of that year some Mk IX and XIX Spitfires. By the end of the year the Squadron was the principal photographic reconnaissance unit in the Far East and had carried out a complete photographic survey of the whole of Indo-China. Moving to Don Muang, Siam in January 1946, they carried out a similar survey of Cambodia.

On 1st September 1946 the Squadron lost its identity when it was moved to Seletar and re-numbered No. 81 Squadron.

A Mission of Mercy

AN EXAMPLE OF WHAT WAS EXPERIENCED by air crews involved in supply-dropping missions from the Cocos Islands is given here by John Behague, formerly of No.99 Squadron. The 14-hour flight he describes was one of the relatively easy ones, but serves to illustrate the tensions, monotony and at times exhilaration that the crews experienced.

Within a very short time of the war ending, men were being returned to the United Kingdom as time-expired or for demobilisation at such an alarming rate that, although the squadrons were fully occupied on ferry duties or the dropping of essential supplies, they were being starved of aircrews to man the aircraft.

John Behague was one of those who volunteered to assist in the crewing of a No.356 Liberator on one such supply dropping mission to Kuala Lumpur on the Malayan Peninsula.

The aircraft were stripped of their guns and armament to provide more lift, and the fitters had installed overload tanks to provide more fuel for the long flight which was routed over many hundreds of miles of the Indian Ocean, far from any other airbase. The bomb bays, which had so recently been used to carry 500 lb and 1,000 lb bombs, were filled with dozens of large drop canisters strapped to parachutes, which were full of essential medical supplies and other comforts for the many prisoners of war and civilian internees who were waiting patiently for the arrival of the main Allied troops.

After a briefing at 0500 hours on Thursday,8th September 1945, we take off at 0630 hours down the uncomfortably short strip hacked from the coconut palms, the wheels screaming as if in agony as they labour along the prefabricated metal runway, the flickering goose-necked flares stretching before us and the palms clearly outlined against the first flush of morning. We are tail heavy and it seems touch-and-go if we will ever leave the deck, but just as the last flare speeds past we creak and grumble upwards, barely airborne and just skimming the beach and reef and then, with the four Pratt and Whitney Twin Wasp engines roaring at full throttle, we slide over the perilously close waves as the pilots tug at the controls, lifting the 15 ton aircraft loaded with nearly 4 tons of supplies into the air.

Visibility is not as perfect as one would have hoped, with banks of black cloud ahead on the horizon as we make the slow, slow climb to cruising altitude. A sparkling sea at first, but as we edge higher it becomes dull and motionless and the thought of several hours of this is somewhat enervating.

After an hour we run into thick cloud and things liven up. Dodging and battling with the stuff can be the most exciting part of flying. There it looms before us, looking as solid and forbidding as a brick wall. We hit it, and it is as silent a collision as diving into cotton wool. Another great cloud bank ahead and this time we slip into it gently with the wings just tobogganing over the top until we are engulfed in torrents of rain and the Liberator is tugged and rocked as if by a giant hand.

A good crew, all nationalities, all jovial. It is difficult to converse except over the intercom because of the noise from the pounding engines. No insulation in these all-metal aircraft. Once you discard your headset you have to shout to make yourself heard. The skipper, a Scot, wanders aft, stepping over mounds of stuff to be parachuted down, checking harnesses, joking and smiling, then sharing pirated flight rations with the rest of us. In the cockpit the Second Dicky pretends to be asleep and lets 'George' (the automatic pilot) take the strain.

Most of us snooze or read novels as the hours creep by. We are all a bit anxious about the performance of our navigator, who has also done his share of nodding. The skipper says this has to be a spot-on mission because there is little fuel in reserve and no room for error.

Then, a cry from up front. Land spotted. It's Sumatra says the navigator, and we lose height to check landmarks. Surprise. Just off the coast a large cargo vessel appears. Its a Jap. With a whoop, Scottie pushes the stick forward and we descend at such speed that we all feel weightless. We are now down to a few hundred feet and lose still more height as we swoop over the ship at mast-top level. A real shoot-up, calculated to shatter the nerves of any Japanese crewman or passengers, but despite the fact that the vessel is under way with funnels steaming, there is no sign of life, no raised faces or fists. Just no response at all. A strange and rather eerie anticlimax.

Back up to a thousand feet and on over Sumatra. Rocky shores then a depressing-looking deeply wooded country; dark green jungle stretching to the horizon. What chance of survival if we have to bale out now? No more, no less I suppose than when we were over the seemingly never-ending ocean.

More shores, more water and Malaya ahead. It's getting warm and humid and we strip off our pullovers and vests and make preparations for the big drop. The coast is in sight. But we have made too early a landfall and are ahead of our ETA – midday – by a good 15 minutes. The skipper throttles back and with engines idling and our ears relaxed we glide onwards with all eyes on the navigator's map. Kuala Lumpur is our destination and the target area is the racetrack.

The civil authorities have been advised to expect us, but it is important to arrive precisely on time so that ground parties will be in position to retrieve the several tons of goodies which will float down.

Watches are consulted, then full throttle again and down we flash, over a desolated coast, skimming palms, then jungle, our objective only a few miles ahead. Maps consulted again.

"Thats the river all right, see how it twists."

The two pilots are tense, the navigator bites his pencil. Any miscalculation now and we'll miss K.L. An attap hut in the distance, then more dwellings, then smoke and suddenly a blur of buildings. We're there! The wireless op reaches for his key and signals to base – "Over target area"

Scottie peruses his special photograph of the area which was pieced together from a combination of shots taken by aircraft on previous sorties. There is a clear sky over the town and we should be able to pinpoint the dropping zone perfectly.

What sights now! The streets seem to be pulsating with life. We're so low that we can see people in white dhoties, in saris, in bright shirts, running and waving their arms. Every house seems to be flying a flag. Union Jacks flutter everywhere. I wonder where they came from? Had they been hidden from the Japanese during the long occupation? We are too fast and too low now to pick out precise details; just a blur of colour.

Up again and we circle the town preparing for our first approach. A green ring to the left. This is it, and we bank in that direction. It's the racecourse, complete with neat-looking pavilion and white rails, just as it is in the picture. Stick forward again and we nose down looking for the reception committee. A man in a grey smock, a priest perhaps, rushes out of the pavilion waving frantically. He's followed by a man in battledress. Then, from nowhere it seems, hundreds of people emerge, all waving, all with mouths open, shouting – men, women, soldiers and scores and scores of children – rushing from the shadows into the sunlight. We wave back from the gun hatches, circle the racetrack then head back to the town centre where we turn and, with flaps fully extended, engine throttled back, make our approach.

In the rear of the Lib we are ready. Bomb doors, cameras and side hatches are open. The bomb aimer in the nose signals his readiness and in we go.

"Revs, revs! We are sinking too quickly, then "Steady, steady!". Throttle back again and we glide in barely 300 feet from the ground. Here comes the racecourse, with crowds falling back. Both pilots are sweating profusely. One air pocket and all will be lost.

"Steady, steady, steady!" Nearer, nearer now, then, "Load gone!"

We shudder upwards and our first batch of containers flutters down. We glance back and see streams of people running to pick up the supplies.

Another circle, another run in, this time catching a group of soldiers unaware and scattering them in all directions as the sudden roar of our engines surprises them. The sight of such a large aircraft flying so low must be a bit mind blowing. Another drop smack in the centre of the green circle, another and another, and that's it. The bomb bays and cargo holds are empty and our mission is complete.

Well, almost... Scottie wants some fun. After his frustrated efforts at shooting up the Japanese freighter he is determined to put on a bit of a show for the people of K.L.

We wave to the crowd at the racecourse and head back to town. Down, down until we seem to be flying between the houses themselves, following and twisting around the streets, missing strings of bunting by inches. The traffic stops, crowds rush out from houses and shops, a great sea of faces stares up from below. Everyone waves. It's an amazing sight to us. What it must seem to them.

There is a Japanese barracks marked on the map, so the pilots decide to pay it a visit. No flags or signs of enthusiasm here. High hats and an occasional flash of teeth. We circle with engines screaming, but no-one in the thin group standing below shows any sign of enthusiasm. One can hardly blame them. A fun fair is in full swing in one part of the town. Victory celebrations no doubt. The children on the roundabouts seem far more concerned with hanging on than of waving to us.

Then suddenly we realise that we are wasting time. We're behind schedule and have many miles to fly to that tiny atoll in the middle of the Indian Ocean. There's an anxious check with watches and fuel gauges and we set course for Cocos. Across the Straits of Malacca, then Sumatra we pound, and finally face the long, long flight across the deep green ocean. The skies have cleared and from 8,000 feet the sea looks beautiful and placid with only the jagged claws of occasional reefs to mar the surface.

Duties complete, most of the crew are lulled to sleep by the drone of the engines. In the cockpit George is switched on and the pilots read, eat and take naps as the controls gently twist and turn to the direction of their robot master. No need to search the skies. The war is over. All Japanese fighters are grounded.

I wake up with muscles cramped to watch the sinking sun. The western sky is suffused in bloody red. It's a gaudy yet glorious picture, like so many one experiences in this part of the world, almost impossible to capture in words, paint or film. Overhead a ceiling of stars unfolds, on either side the bright pinpricks of our navigation lights stare back. Below, cloud is forming, fleecy white at first, but ahead and approaching fast are grey, forbidding banks.

On, on, on, with the engines roaring a robust song, the coldness of night beginning to seep into the aircraft. 5pm comes and goes, six o'clock, seven and still the clouds surround us, much blacker now but occasional windows opening to the dark ocean and the stars. All the crew are awake, alert, anxious and tired. We strain our eyes for some sign of the lonely island which is our temporary home and refuge.

The petrol gauges indicate enough fuel for a few minutes only. We have been on radio compass for the past hour. Is it servicable?

"Nav, are you sure we're on track? Try another DF bearing."

The navigator is adamant but has a worried look.

"Any minute now," he says.

The bearing remains steady. More minutes pass. The tanks must surely soon be dry. Thoughts race through my mind. The war's over, so what on earth possessed me to volunteer for this trip. So near and yet (looking at gauges now fluttering in the red) so far. I feel empty too and slightly sick and quite clearly so do the others.

Then, far away in the dark distance, a tiny light, then the steady finger of a searchlight reveals itself like a beam from heaven. It can only be Cocos. Home at last! Everyone relaxes. We grin, yawn, stretch limbs, gather our belongings. Soon the flarepath is ahead.

Undercart down. Landing stations are taken up. No time for a circuit. A quick word with the control tower and straight in. Harnesses are snapped off as we hit the deck and roar down the strip, blue flames from glowing exhausts reflecting against the sides of the Lib.

They are all waiting for us at dispersal and rush out to help, clasping hands and asking whether we'd found out target and delivered the goods.

"Good show," says the Intelligence officer.

There's just time for a mug of hot tea, supper for those who want it, then off to out tents and our charpoys (beds). It has been a long day.

APPENDIX 3

IN MEMORIAM

A Liberator takes off from the steel airstrip on the Cocos Islands, 1945.

WITH THE MARCH OF TIME, the names of those who died while serving in some distant outpost of Empire are soon forgotten – except perhaps during the lifetime of their families and those who served with them. When the Royal Air Force abandoned the Cocos Islands as a base in 1946, the bodies of those who died and were buried on the islands were removed and re-interred in the War Graves Cemetery at Kranji, Singapore.

For over 50 years there remained no trace of these men on the islands until Harry Widdup, who was a member of the Royal New Zealand Air Force and served as a Flight Engineer on C87 Skymasters with No.232 Squadron and made many overnight stops on the Islands during 1945/6, decided that, to mark the 50th Anniversary of the ending of World War 2, a memorial ought to be erected to the memory of the crew of Liberator EW622 of No.232 Squadron who lost their lives when the aircraft crashed on taking off from the Cocos Islands on the 30th August 1945.

On commencing to obtain details of the crash and the names of the crew members he found that there were many more men who had lost their lives while serving on the islands and no tangible evidence remained of their passing. With a group of enthusiasts and with the assistance of many organisations and individuals he obtained the details of over 60 men who had lost their lives on the islands, including aircrew who had failed to return from operations during and after the war. He decided that a permanent memorial should be erected to their memory.

On Anzac Day 1995, members of the Royal New Zealand Air Force carried out a wreath laying memorial ceremony on West Island in memory of the Royal Australian Air Force Pilot of Liberator EW622 and his crew. On the 6th June 1995 members of the Royal New Zealand Air Force brought to the Islands a Book and Roll of Honour, Memorial Cross and Wreaths. The 19th June saw the result of the dedication of Harry Widdup and his friends when the Commanding Officer of No.5 Squadron Royal New Zealand Air Force flew to the Cocos Islands bring with him a Padre from the RNZAF Base at Whenuapai who conducted a Service of Remembrance attended by all those living on the islands and many members of the Royal Australian Air Force who are stationed there.

The Roll of Honour is still being added to and records by page the Names, Rank, Number, Trade,, Unit, Age, Date of Death Cause of Death, Next of Kin and the place of Burial or Memorial if known. The Cross is of stainless steel and stands some 500mm high and 400mm wide. The setting consists of a central Monument fenced with white painted steel railings topped with 'Fleur-de-Lys' approximately one metre high with a gate in the left hand corner. The compound is approximately five metres square with a gravel garden bordered with concrete. At the rear are three further monuments. The centre one is inscribed; 'Erected by members of No.2 Airfield Construction Squadron, Royal Australian Air Force in memory of; Michael Paul Rowan, Leading Aircraftman RAAF, Peter James Eccleston Aircraftman RAAF, and John Emery Atkinson, Able Seaman RN. The Aircraftmen lost their lives in an heroic attempt by members of 2.A.C.S. to rescue Atkinson and four members of the Royal Navy Marines and Royal Engineers who were in danger of drowning beyond the reef off this point on Sunday 6th April 1952.

The left rear monument is inscribed:

Erected in memory of:

LAC Weir, V.E.D. 129 SP

AC2 Ward, C.W.

Died on Active Service June 1945.

AC1 Mansfield, H.P.

LAC Peales, T.P.

LAC Vennier, A.
Sgt. Simmonds, E.
F/Sgt Hopwood, F.
June 1945.

The centre rear monument is inscribed;
In memory of the crew of
Catalina JX435.
Died 27th June 1945.
W/O Freeman.
F/Sgts Paramore, Marshall, Denmark & Spearing
Cpl Haworth
LAC Butler

The rear right monument is inscribed;
Erected to the memory of the crew of Liberator EW622 (232 Squadron), Missing believed killed, 30th August 1945.
F/O R.G. Sweetman
F/O B.E.C. Ford
F/0 W.U.J. Dearlove
F/Lt S.D. Goldworthy
Sgt K.J. Deery

A list of those killed or missing while serving or operating from the Cocos Island is recorded in the Book of Remembrance and is still being added to and includes the crews of;

356 Squadron Liberator – KL.654. Lost on 23/8/1945.

356 Squadron Liberator – KH.213. Lost on 18/8/1945.   *218*

356 Squadron Liberator – Missing on 23/8/1945.

99 Squadron Liberator – Crashed Palambang

99 Squadron Liberator – Missing 7/10/1945.

Also F/O John Lawson McBride, 356 Squadron, Navigator, killed during an attack on a Japanese Airfield on 7/8/1945 - the last bombing raid of the war and F/O J.A. Law DFC, F/Sgt D.E. Olden, F/Sgt G.T. Watkins & Sgt P. West, all of No.203 Squadron who were killed when their Liberator was shot down during an attack on a Japanese ship in the Sunda Straits.